D0790089

Avenue
Q

The Musical

The Applause Libretto Library Series

Avenue

The Musical

The Complete Book and Lyrics
of the Broadway Musical

Music and Lyrics by Robert Lopez and Jeff Marx

Book by Jeff Whitty

**Based on an Original Concept
by Robert Lopez and Jeff Marx**

APPLAUSE
THEATRE & CINEMA BOOKS

An Imprint of Hal Leonard Corporation

Music and Lyrics by Robert Lopez and Jeff Marx Copyright © 2003 Only For Now, Inc. and Fantasies Come True, Inc. (administered by Warner-Tamerlane Publishing Corp.). International Copyright Secured. All Rights Reserved.

Book by Jeff Whitty Copyright © 2003. International Copyright Secured. All Rights Reserved.

All rights reserved. No part of this book may be reproduced in any form, without written permission, except by a newspaper or magazine reviewer who wishes to quote brief passages in connection with a review.

Published in 2010 by Applause Theatre & Cinema Books
An Imprint of Hal Leonard Corporation
7777 West Bluemound Road
Milwaukee, WI 53213

Trade Book Division Editorial Offices
33 Plymouth St., Montclair, NJ 07042

Please be aware that this copy of *Avenue Q* is not to be used for rehearsal purposes. If you wish to produce a production of all or any portion of the Play (including any workshop, reading, concert version, or any revue containing selections from *Avenue Q* that includes staging and/ or props), you must obtain permission in the form of a written license from the Play's exclusive dramatic performing rights licensing agent, Music Theatre International (MTI), 421 West 54th Street, New York, NY 10019 (tel. 212-541-4684 or www.mtishows.com). MTI also provides all materials necessary to produce the Play, including a production script. Please also be aware that ASCAP, BMI and SESAC are prohibited from licensing dramatic performing rights in *Avenue Q*. A license from such companies will not authorize you to produce any dramatic performance of the Play or any scenes or songs from the Play.

***Avenue Q* is fully protected under the copyright laws of the United States of America and all countries of the Berne and Universal Copyright Conventions. PERFORMING ANY PORTION OF *AVENUE Q* WITHOUT A WRITTEN LICENSE FROM THE AUTHORS OR THEIR REPRESENTATIVES MAY SUBJECT YOU TO PENALTIES UNDER U.S. AND INTERNATIONAL COPYRIGHT LAW.**

The Authors strictly reserve all rights in *Avenue Q*, including all professional, amateur, classroom, reading and workshop performances, publication, motion picture, radio, television, Internet and similar rights, and the right to adapt and translate the Play. Anyone wishing to make any use of the Play must secure written permission from the Authors. No portion of the Play may be duplicated, published in any publication or uploaded to the Internet.

Printed in the United States of America
Book design by Mark Lerner

Library of Congress Cataloging-in-Publication Data is available upon request.
ISBN 978-1-4234-8904-7

www.applausepub.com

CONTENTS

CAST AND CREDITS

Avenue Q

Original 2003 Broadway Company

Princeton / Rod: John Tartaglia
Kate Monster / Lucy the Slut: Stephanie D'Abruzzo
Trekkie Monster, Nicky, Boy Bear: Rick Lyon
Gary Coleman: Natalie Venetia Belcon
Brian: Jordan Gelber
Christmas Eve: Ann Harada
Mrs. Thistletwat, Girl Bear: Jennifer Barnhart

Director: Jason Moore
Set: Anna Louizos
Lighting: Howell Binkley
Costume Design: Mirena Rada
Choreography: Ken Roberson
Musical Supervision, Orchestration and Arrangements: Stephen
  Oremus
Puppet Design: Rick Lyon

Avenue Q was developed at the Eugene O'Neill Musical Theater
Conference in 2002. It opened Off-Broadway as a co-production of
the New Group and the Vineyard Theater on March 20, 2003. It then
moved to Broadway's Golden Theater, opening on July 31, 2003.

Subsequent productions included Las Vegas in September 2005 and London's West End in June 2006. Two U.S. national tours also followed as well as dozens of international productions in countries as diverse as Brazil, Israel, Finland, the Philippines, Australia, Hungary, Turkey, Mexico, Sweden, Spain, and Italy. The Broadway production closed on September 13, 2009, and moved Off-Broadway to New World Stages on October 9, 2009, where it still runs as of this writing.

Avenue Q won three 2004 Tony Awards: Best Musical, Best Score (Robert Lopez and Jeff Marx), and Best Book (Jeff Whitty).

CHARACTERS

PUPPET CHARACTERS

Princeton, a fresh-faced kid just out of college

Kate Monster, a kindergarten teaching assistant, a bit older than Princeton

Nicky, a bit of a slacker, who lives with

Rod, a Republican investment banker with a secret

Trekkie Monster, a reclusive creature obsessed with the Internet

Lucy, a vixen-ish vamp with a dangerous edge

The Bad Idea Bears, two snuggly, cute teddy-bear types

Mrs. T., ancient, Kate's boss

HUMAN CHARACTERS

Brian, a laid-back guy engaged to

Christmas Eve, a therapist who moved here from Japan

Gary Coleman. Yes, that Gary Coleman. He lives on the Avenue, too. He's the superintendent.

Note: Christmas Eve speaks with a subtle Japanese dialect. In instances where hitting the dialect is necessary to make a point, comic or otherwise, it's noted in the script.

SCENES

ACT ONE

ACT TWO

MUSICAL NUMBERS

ACT ONE

"The Avenue Q Theme"	Company
"What Do You Do with a B.A. in English?"	Princeton
"It Sucks to Be Me"	Kate Monster, Brian, Nicky, Rod, Christmas Eve, Gary Coleman, Princeton
"If You Were Gay"	Nicky and Rod
"Purpose"	Princeton, Moving Boxes
"Everyone's a Little Bit Racist"	Kate Monster, Princeton, Gary Coleman, Brian, Christmas Eve
"The Internet Is for Porn"	Kate Monster, Trekkie Monster, Brian, Rod, Gary Coleman, Princeton
"Mix Tape"	Kate and Princeton
"I'm Not Wearing Underwear Today"	Brian
"Special"	Lucy the Slut

MUSICAL NUMBERS

Avenue Q

The Musical

A WARNING FROM THE PUPPET POLICE

The purchase of this script does not authorize the performance of all or any part of *Avenue Q*, whether or not such performance is for a paying audience. Performance of *Avenue Q*, including rehearsals, requires permission from the copyright holders and a written performance license, which may be obtained from Music Theatre International, 421 West 54th St., New York, NY 10019 (tel. 212-541-4684 or www.mtishows.com). If you believe this script is being used in an unauthorized production, please call MTI at the number above or email licensing@mtishows.com.

Act One

SCENE 1—INTRO / GRADUATION / ON THE AVENUE

(*An overture, with accompanying video.*)

VOICES

THE SUN IS SHINING, IT'S A LOVELY DAY,
A PERFECT MORNING FOR A KID TO PLAY,
BUT YOU'VE GOT LOTS OF BILLS TO PAY—
WHAT CAN YOU DO?
YOU WORK REAL HARD AND THE PAY'S REAL LOW,
AND EV'RY HOUR GOES OH SO SLOW,
AND AT THE END OF THE DAY THERE'S NOWHERE TO GO
BUT HOME TO AVENUE Q! YOU LIVE ON AVENUE Q!
YOUR FRIENDS DO TOO.
YOU ARE TWENTY-TWO AND YOU LIVE ON AVENUE Q!
YOU LIVE ON AVENUE Q.
YOU LIVE ON AVENUE Q!

(PRINCETON *appears, in a graduation cap.*)

PRINCETON

WHAT DO YOU DO WITH A B.A. IN ENGLISH?
WHAT IS MY LIFE GOING TO BE?
FOUR YEARS OF COLLEGE AND PLENTY OF KNOWLEDGE

HAVE EARNED ME THIS USELESS DEGREE.
I CAN'T PAY THE BILLS YET
'CAUSE I HAVE NO SKILLS YET.
THE WORLD IS A BIG, SCARY PLACE.
BUT SOMEHOW I CAN'T SHAKE
THE FEELING I MIGHT MAKE
A DIFFERENCE TO THE HUMAN RACE!

(*Lights rise on Avenue Q, a homey, dilapidated street in an outer-outer borough of New York City. On one building hangs a sign: "Apartment for Rent."*)

(BRIAN *is putting some garbage out on the street.* KATE MONSTER *enters.*)

KATE MONSTER

Morning, Brian!

BRIAN

Hi, Kate Monster.

KATE MONSTER

How's life?

BRIAN

Disappointing!

KATE MONSTER

What's the matter?

BRIAN

The catering company laid me off.

KATE MONSTER

I'm sorry!

BRIAN

Me too! I mean, look at me! I'm ten years out of college, and I always thought—

(*He stops.*)

KATE MONSTER

What?

BRIAN

No, it sounds stupid.

KATE MONSTER

Come on!

BRIAN

(*Sings.*)
WHEN I WAS LITTLE
I THOUGHT I WOULD BE—

KATE MONSTER

What?

BRIAN

A BIG COMEDIAN ON LATE NIGHT TV.
BUT NOW I'M THIRTY-TWO AND AS YOU CAN SEE
I'M NOT. OH WELL,
IT SUCKS TO BE ME.
IT SUCKS TO BE ME.
IT SUCKS TO BE BROKE AND UNEMPLOYED

AND TURNING THIRTY-THREE.
IT SUCKS TO BE ME!

KATE MONSTER

Oh, you think your life sucks?

BRIAN

I think so.

KATE MONSTER

Your problems aren't so bad!
     (*Sings.*)
I'M KINDA PRETTY
AND PRETTY DAMN SMART.

BRIAN

You are.

KATE MONSTER

Thanks!
I LIKE ROMANTIC THINGS LIKE MUSIC AND ART
AND AS YOU KNOW I HAVE A GIGANTIC HEART,
SO WHY
DON'T I HAVE A BOYFRIEND?
FUCK!
IT SUCKS TO BE ME!

BRIAN

Me too.

KATE MONSTER

IT SUCKS TO BE ME.

BRIAN

IT SUCKS TO BE ME.
IT SUCKS TO BE BRIAN—

KATE MONSTER

AND KATE—

BRIAN

TO NOT HAVE A JOB—

KATE MONSTER

TO NOT HAVE A DATE!

BOTH

IT SUCKS TO BE ME.

(ROD *and* NICKY *enter, arguing.*)

BRIAN

Oh, Nicky, Rod—can you settle something for us? Do you have a second?

ROD

Certainly.

KATE MONSTER

Whose life sucks more? Brian's or mine?

(NICKY *and* ROD *exchange a look.*)

NICKY AND ROD

Ours!

ROD

WE LIVE TOGETHER.

NICKY

WE'RE CLOSE AS PEOPLE CAN GET.

ROD

WE'VE BEEN THE BEST OF BUDDIES—

NICKY

EVER SINCE THE DAY WE MET.

ROD

SO HE KNOWS LOTS OF WAYS TO MAKE ME REALLY UPSET.
OH, EVERY DAY IS AN AGGRAVATION!

NICKY

COME ON, THAT'S AN EXAGGERATION!

ROD

YOU LEAVE YOUR CLOTHES OUT.
YOU PUT YOUR FEET ON MY CHAIR.

NICKY

Oh yeah?
YOU DO SUCH ANAL THINGS
LIKE IRONING YOUR UNDERWEAR.

ROD

YOU MAKE THAT VERY SMALL APARTMENT WE SHARE
A HELL!

NICKY

SO DO YOU,
THAT'S WHY I'M IN HELL TOO!

ROD

IT SUCKS TO BE ME!

NICKY

IT SUCKS TO BE ME!

KATE MONSTER

IT SUCKS TO BE ME!

BRIAN

IT SUCKS TO BE ME!

ALL

IS THERE ANYBODY HERE IT DOESN'T SUCK TO BE?
IT SUCKS TO BE ME!

(*A dance break.*)

KATE MONSTER

DA DA DA DA DA—

BRIAN

DA DA DA DA DA—

NICKY

DA DA DA DAA DAA—

ROD

DA DA DA DA.

(CHRISTMAS EVE *pops her head out of a window.*)

CHRISTMAS EVE
Brian! What you doing?

BRIAN
Oh shit.

(*She closes the window.* BRIAN *shrugs and keeps dancing.*)

KATE MONSTER
DA DA DA DA DA—

BRIAN
DA DA DA DA DA—

NICKY
DA DA DA DAA DAA—

ROD
DA DA DA DA.

CHRISTMAS EVE
Why you all so happy?

NICKY
Because our lives suck!

CHRISTMAS EVE
Your lives suck? I hearing you correctly? Ha!
I COMING TO THIS COUNTRY
FOR OPPORTUNITIES.

TRIED TO WORK IN KOREAN DELI
BUT I AM JAPANESE.
BUT WITH HARD WORK I EARN
TWO MASTER'S DEGREES
IN SOCIAL WORK!
AND NOW I AM THERAPIST!
BUT I HAVE NO CLIENTS!
    (*Smacking* BRIAN.)
AND I HAVE AN UNEMPLOYED FIANCÉ!
AND WE HAVE LOTS OF BILLS TO PAY!
IT SUCK TO BE ME!
IT SUCK TO BE ME!
I SAY IT
SUCKA-SUCKA-SUCKA-SUCKA-SUCKA-SUCKA-SUCKA-SUCKA
SUCKA-SUCKA-SUCKA-SUCKA
SUCK!
IT SUCK TO BE ME.

    (PRINCETON *enters*.)

PRINCETON

Excuse me?

BRIAN

Hey there.

PRINCETON

Sorry to bother you, but I'm looking for a place to live.

CHRISTMAS EVE

Why you looking all the way out here?

PRINCETON

Well, I started at Avenue A, but everything so far is out of my price range. But this neighborhood looks a lot cheaper! Oh, and look—here's a "For Rent" sign!

BRIAN

You need to talk to the superintendent. Let me get him.

PRINCETON

Oh, thanks.

BRIAN

Gary!

GARY COLEMAN

I'm comin'! I'm comin'!

(GARY COLEMAN *appears, dramatically, on the fire escape.*)

PRINCETON

Oh my God! It's Gary Coleman!

GARY COLEMAN

Yes, I am!
I'M GARY COLEMAN
FROM TV'S *DIFF'RENT STROKES*
I MADE A LOTTA MONEY THAT GOT
STOLEN BY MY FOLKS!
NOW I'M BROKE AND I'M THE BUTT
OF EVERYONE'S JOKES,
BUT I'M HERE—
The superintendent!
ON AVENUE Q—

ALL

IT SUCKS TO BE YOU.

KATE MONSTER

You win!

ALL

IT SUCKS TO BE YOU.

BRIAN

I feel better now!

GARY COLEMAN

TRY HAVING PEOPLE STOPPING YOU TO ASK YOU
"What you talkin' 'bout, Willis?"
> (*Beat.*)
It gets old.

ALL

IT SUCKS TO BE YOU.
ON AVENUE Q. (SUCKS TO BE ME)
ON AVENUE Q. (SUCKS TO BE YOU)
ON AVENUE Q. (SUCKS TO BE US)
BUT NOT WHEN WE'RE TOGETHER!
WE'RE TOGETHER HERE
ON AVENUE Q,
WE LIVE ON AVENUE Q—
OUR FRIENDS DO TOO!
TILL OUR DREAMS COME TRUE
WE LIVE ON AVENUE Q.

PRINCETON

This is real life!

ALL

WE LIVE ON AVENUE Q.

NICKY

You're gonna love it.

ALL

WE LIVE ON AVENUE Q.

GARY COLEMAN

Here's your keys!

ALL

WELCOME TO AVENUE Q!

(*Music ends.* NICKY *and* ROD *exit.*)

BRIAN

So what's your name?

PRINCETON

I'm Princeton.

BRIAN

Hey, buddy, I'm Brian. This is my fiancée.

CHRISTMAS EVE

My name Christmas Eve. You so cute! Very handsome! You single?

PRINCETON

Yeah—

CHRISTMAS EVE
(*Pointing at* KATE.)
Because she single.

KATE MONSTER
(*Embarrassed*.)
Oh, Christmas Eve!

BRIAN
That's Kate Monster. She lives in our building.

PRINCETON
Hi—

KATE MONSTER
Hi!

(TREKKIE MONSTER's *window flies open. He throws a bag of trash outside, which lands with a "thud" on the sidewalk.*)

GARY COLEMAN
Trekkie!

BRIAN
Good morning, Trekkie!

TREKKIE MONSTER
Me no time to talk. Me busy.

(*He slams the window shut.*)

BRIAN
And that's Trekkie Monster.

CHRISTMAS EVE

He a pervert. You no spending time with him.

GARY COLEMAN

Come on inside, kid. I'll show you the place.

PRINCETON

Great!

(*As they exit—*)

GARY COLEMAN

You know, many distinguished people have expressed interest in this fine address.

PRINCETON

No kidding!

GARY COLEMAN

Mmm-hmm!

(*They're gone.*)

CHRISTMAS EVE

So what you think, Kate Monster? He cute, right?

KATE MONSTER

Yeah—

CHRISTMAS EVE

You go get him! A man respond to an aggressive woman.
        (*To* BRIAN, *pushing him.*)
You! Go get job!

BRIAN

I'll get right on it!

(*He jogs off.*)

CHRISTMAS EVE

(*To* KATE.)

See?

(CHRISTMAS EVE *goes inside.* KATE *glances toward where* PRINCETON *exited, and then follows her.*)

SCENE 2—NICKY AND ROD'S APARTMENT

(ROD *sits in his tasteful apartment, with a book.*)

ROD

Ah, an afternoon alone with my favorite book, *Broadway Musicals of the 1940s.* No roommate to bother me. How can it get any better than this?

(NICKY *enters cheerfully.*)

NICKY

Oh, hi, Rod!

ROD

Hi, Nicky.

NICKY

Hey, Rod, you'll never guess what happened to me on the subway this morning. This guy was smiling at me and talking to me—

                              ROD

That's very interesting.

                             NICKY

He was being real friendly, and you know, I think he was coming on to me. I think he might've thought I was gay!

                              ROD
      (*Uncomfortable.*)
Ahem, so, uh, why are you telling me this? Why should I care? I don't care. What did you have for lunch today?

                             NICKY

Rod, there's no need to get—

                              ROD

I'm not getting defensive! What do I care about some gay guy you met? I'm trying to read.

      (*A moment.* ROD *returns to his book.*)

                             NICKY

Oh, I didn't mean anything by it, Rod. I just think it's something we should be able to talk about.

                              ROD

I don't want to talk about it! Nicky, this conversation is over!
      (*Beat.*)
Over!

                             NICKY

Well, okay, but just so you know—
IF YOU WERE GAY,

THAT'D BE OKAY.
I MEAN 'CUZ, HEY
I'D LIKE YOU ANYWAY.
BECAUSE YOU SEE
IF IT WERE ME
I WOULD FEEL FREE
TO SAY
THAT I WAS GAY
(BUT I'M NOT GAY).

ROD

Nicky, please! I'm trying to read. . . .
　　(NICKY *stares at him.*)
What?!

NICKY	**ROD**
IF YOU WERE QUEER	Nicky—
I'D STILL BE HERE	Nicky, I'm trying to read this book.
YEAR AFTER YEAR	Nicky—
BECAUSE YOU'RE DEAR	
TO ME	Argh!
AND I KNOW THAT YOU	What?
WOULD ACCEPT ME TOO	I would?
IF I TOLD YOU TODAY	
HEY, GUESS WHAT,	
I'M GAY	
(BUT I'M NOT GAY).	
I'M HAPPY	
JUST BEING WITH YOU	*High Button Shoes, Pal Joey* . . .
SO WHAT SHOULD IT MATTER TO ME	
WHAT YOU DO IN BED WITH	
GUYS?	Nicky, that's *gross*!

NICKY	ROD
NO, IT'S NOT!	
IF YOU WERE GAY	Awwh!
I'D SHOUT HOORAY!	I'm not listening!
AND HERE I'D STAY	La la la la la!
BUT I WOULDN'T GET IN YOUR	
WAY.	Aaaah!
YOU CAN COUNT ON ME	
TO ALWAYS BE	
BESIDE YOU EVERY DAY	
TO TELL YOU IT'S OKAY,	
YOU WERE JUST BORN THAT WAY,	
AND AS THEY SAY,	
IT'S IN YOUR DNA,	
YOU'RE GAY!	I'M NOT GAAAAY!

NICKY

If you were gay.

ROD

Argh!

SCENE 3—PRINCETON'S APARTMENT

(GARY *brings in some packing boxes and a stack of envelopes.* PRINCETON *follows.*)

PRINCETON

Hey, Gary, thanks for helping me move in!

GARY COLEMAN

No sweat! And look—you got your first day of mail!

PRINCETON

Oh, thanks!

GARY COLEMAN

What's in all these boxes? Anything good?

PRINCETON

My parents sent all of my stuff from home!

GARY COLEMAN

How nice! And you also got your rent bill, your utility bill, your student loan bill, your credit card bill, your Internet bill, your cell phone bill—

PRINCETON

Oh my God!

GARY COLEMAN

You got any money?

PRINCETON

Well, I start work tomorrow—

(*The phone rings.* GARY *picks it up.*)

GARY COLEMAN

Gary Coleman.
        (*To* PRINCETON.)
It's for you.

(*He hands the phone to* PRINCETON.)

PRINCETON

(*We hear pandemonium on the other end of the line.*)

Um, hello?—Oh, hi!

(*Excitedly, to* GARY.)

It's my job!

(*On phone.*)

I can't wait to meet all of you tomorrow—. Sorry, I can barely hear you—. Uh-huh. Uh, did you say "downsizing"? But how can I be laid off when I haven't even—no, please don't hang up! Please! *How am I supposed to live?*

(*The line goes dead.*)

Hello?

GARY COLEMAN

Oh, kid, don't look so long in the face. Here's a bit of advice: never underestimate the power of long-range planning. If life gets you down, don't sit on your ass and let it pass you by. 'Cause you know what they say—if you rearrange the letters in the word "unemployed," it spells "opportunity"!

PRINCETON

What?

(GARY *smiles and exits.*)

PRINCETON

Maybe this *is* an opportunity! Maybe I'm not meant to work in some dumb office for the rest of my life! Maybe—maybe I have a higher purpose!

(*Suddenly, the video screen springs to life with an animated instructional video.*)

CHILD'S VOICE

What's a purpose?

VOICE

A purpose is direction to your life. It could be a job, a family, it could be the pursuit of knowledge or wealth. Everybody's purpose is different. The best thing about a purpose is that it gives your life meaning.

CHILD'S VOICE

I want a purpose!

PRINCETON

(*Sings.*)
PURPOSE:
IT'S THAT LITTLE FLAME
THAT LIGHTS A FIRE
UNDER YOUR ASS.
PURPOSE:
IT KEEPS YOU GOING STRONG
LIKE A CAR WITH A FULL TANK OF GAS.
EVERYONE ELSE HAS A PURPOSE,
SO WHAT'S MINE?
(*He picks a penny up off the ground.*)
Oh, look! Here's a penny! It's from the year I was born!
IT'S A SIGN!
I DON'T KNOW HOW I KNOW
BUT I'M GONNA FIND MY PURPOSE.
I DON'T KNOW WHERE I'M GONNA LOOK
BUT I'M GONNA FIND MY PURPOSE.
GOTTA FIND OUT, DON'T WANNA WAIT!
GOT TO MAKE SURE THAT MY LIFE WILL BE GREAT!
GOTTA FIND MY PURPOSE
BEFORE IT'S TOO LATE!

(*His moving boxes join in.*)

MOVING BOXES AND OTHERS
HE'S GONNA FIND HIS PURPOSE!

PRINCETON
I'M GONNA FIND MY PURPOSE!

MOVING BOXES AND OTHERS
HE'S GONNA FIND HIS PURPOSE!

PRINCETON
I'M GONNA FIND MY PURPOSE!
COULD BE FAR, COULD BE NEAR,
COULD TAKE A WEEK, A MONTH, A YEAR.
AT A JOB, OR SMOKING GRASS—
MAYBE AT A POTTERY CLASS!
COULD IT BE? YES IT COULD!
SOMETHING'S COMING, SOMETHING GOOD!
I'M GONNA FIND MY PURPOSE!

MOVING BOXES AND OTHERS
YOU'RE GONNA FIND YOUR PURPOSE!

PRINCETON
I'M GONNA FIND MY PURPOSE—
I'M GONNA FIND IT!
WHAT WILL IT BE? WHERE WILL IT BE?
MY PURPOSE IN LIFE IS A MYSTERY.
GOTTA FIND MY PURPOSE—
GOTTA FIND ME.
I'M GONNA FIND MY PURPOSE!
PURPOSE PURPOSE PURPOSE!
YEAH YEAH!
I GOTTA FIND ME.

(Applause, playoff.)

MOVING BOXES

HE'S GONNA FIND HIS PURPOSE

WHOA, WHOA, WHOA . . .

SCENE 4—ON THE AVENUE

(On the video screen: the word "PURPOSE.")

(CHRISTMAS EVE *appears.*)

CHRISTMAS EVE

My purpose in life is to help people find themselves.

(She disappears. BRIAN *appears.)*

BRIAN

My purpose in life is to make people laugh. And make money doing it.

(BRIAN *disappears.* GARY *appears.*)

GARY COLEMAN

My greatest fear is that I already achieved my damn purpose in life. And now I'm just happy to walk out my front door with a little bit of self-respect.

(GARY *disappears. Lights up on the Avenue, where* PRINCETON *stands.*)

(KATE MONSTER *enters.*)

PRINCETON

Oh—hey, Kate Monster!

KATE MONSTER

Princeton! Hi!

PRINCETON

Say, Kate—can I ask you a question?

KATE MONSTER

Sure!

PRINCETON

What's your purpose in life?

KATE MONSTER

Oh! Well—I'm a kindergarten teaching assistant.

PRINCETON

Right. But what's your purpose? Your dream! Your mission!

KATE MONSTER

Nobody ever wants to know that!

PRINCETON

I do!

KATE MONSTER

(*Blushing.*)
Well, since you asked—No, I can't! I barely know you!

PRINCETON

Awww, come on!

KATE MONSTER

Okay.

    (*Over tinkling music.*)

When I was a little Monster, I always wished I had a special place I could go. A special school, only for Monsters. The media only talks about the bad things Monsters do, but some of the most productive members of our society are People of Fur. So my dream is to start a special school, only for Monsters, where little Monsters can become part of the global community. So that, in short, is my purpose.

    (*Music ends. Beat.*)

But I'm not an egghead! I like to have fun, and party—

PRINCETON

So you're, like, all into Monster stuff!

KATE MONSTER

Uh-huh.

PRINCETON

Do you know Trekkie Monster upstairs?

KATE MONSTER

Uh-huh!

PRINCETON

Well, he's Trekkie Monster, and you're Kate Monster.

KATE MONSTER

Right.

PRINCETON

You're both Monsters.

KATE MONSTER

Yeah.

PRINCETON

Are you two related?

KATE MONSTER

(*Shocked.*)
What? Princeton, I'm surprised at you! I find that racist!

PRINCETON

I'm sorry! I was just asking.

KATE MONSTER

Well, it's a touchy subject. No, not all Monsters are related. What are you trying to say—that we all look the same to you?

PRINCETON

No, not at all. I'm sorry, I guess that was a little racist.

KATE MONSTER

I should say so. You should be much more careful when you're talking about the sensitive subject of race.

PRINCETON

Well, look who's talking!

KATE MONSTER

What do you mean?

PRINCETON

What about that special Monster school you just told me about?

KATE MONSTER
What about it?

PRINCETON
Could someone like me go there?

KATE MONSTER
No, we don't want people like you—

(*She gasps.*)

PRINCETON
You see!?
(*Sings.*)
YOU'RE A LITTLE BIT RACIST.

KATE MONSTER
WELL, YOU'RE A LITTLE BIT TOO!

PRINCETON
I GUESS WE'RE BOTH A LITTLE BIT RACIST—

KATE MONSTER
ADMITTING IT IS NOT AN EASY THING TO DO—

PRINCETON
BUT I GUESS IT'S TRUE—

KATE MONSTER
BETWEEN ME AND YOU,
I THINK

BOTH

EVERYONE'S A LITTLE BIT RACIST SOMETIMES.
DOESN'T MEAN WE GO AROUND COMMITTING HATE CRIMES.
LOOK AROUND AND YOU WILL FIND
NO ONE'S REALLY COLOR-BLIND.
MAYBE IT'S A FACT WE ALL SHOULD FACE.
EVERYONE MAKES JUDGMENTS . . .
BASED ON RACE!

PRINCETON

Not big judgments, like who to hire or who to buy a newspaper from.

KATE MONSTER

No!

PRINCETON

No, just little judgments, like thinking that Mexican busboys should learn to speak goddamn English!

KATE MONSTER

Right!

BOTH

EVERYONE'S A LITTLE BIT RACIST—TODAY.
SO, EVERYONE'S A LITTLE BIT RACIST—OKAY.
ETHNIC JOKES MIGHT BE UNCOUTH
BUT YOU LAUGH BECAUSE THEY'RE BASED ON TRUTH!
DON'T TAKE THEM AS PERSONAL ATTACKS
EVERYONE ENJOYS THEM—
SO RELAX!

PRINCETON

All right, stop me if you've heard this one. There's a plane going down and there's only one parachute. And there's a rabbi, a priest—

KATE MONSTER

And a *black* guy!

(GARY COLEMAN *pops out from behind the fence.*)

GARY COLEMAN

Whatchoo talkin' about, Kate?

KATE MONSTER

Uh—

GARY COLEMAN

You were telling a *black* joke!

PRINCETON

Well, yeah, Gary, but lots of people tell black jokes . . .

GARY COLEMAN

I don't.

PRINCETON

Of course you don't. You're *black*! But I bet you tell Polack jokes, right?

GARY COLEMAN

Sure I do.
        (*He busts up, laughing.*)
Those stupid Polacks!

PRINCETON

Don't you think that's a little racist?

GARY COLEMAN

Well, damn, I guess you're right.

KATE MONSTER

YOU'RE A LITTLE BIT RACIST.

GARY COLEMAN

WELL, YOU'RE A LITTLE BIT TOO.

PRINCETON

WE'RE ALL A LITTLE BIT RACIST.

GARY COLEMAN

I THINK THAT I WOULD HAVE TO AGREE WITH YOU.

PRINCETON AND KATE MONSTER

WE'RE GLAD YOU DO,

GARY COLEMAN

IT'S SAD, BUT TRUE!
EVERYONE'S A LITTLE BIT RACIST—
ALL RIGHT!

KATE MONSTER

ALL RIGHT!

PRINCETON

ALL RIGHT!

GARY COLEMAN

ALL RIGHT!!
BIGOTRY HAS NEVER BEEN EXCLUSIVELY WHITE—

ALL

IF WE ALL COULD JUST ADMIT
THAT WE ARE RACIST A LITTLE BIT
EVEN THOUGH WE ALL KNOW THAT IT'S WRONG
MAYBE IT WOULD HELP US
GET ALONG!

PRINCETON

Christ, do I feel good!

GARY COLEMAN

Now there was a fine upstanding black man!

PRINCETON

Who?

GARY COLEMAN

Jesus Christ!

KATE MONSTER

But, Gary, Jesus was white!

GARY COLEMAN

No, Jesus was black.

KATE MONSTER

No, Jesus was white!

GARY COLEMAN

No, I'm pretty sure Jesus was black!

PRINCETON

Guys—Jesus was Jewish!

(*They all laugh.* BRIAN *enters.*)

BRIAN

Hey guys, what are you laughing about?

GARY COLEMAN

Racism!

BRIAN

Cool!

(CHRISTMAS EVE *enters.*)

CHRISTMAS EVE

Brian! You come back here! You take out lecycuraburs!

PRINCETON

What's that mean?

BRIAN

Um. Recyclables.
(*Everyone laughs.*)
Hey! Don't laugh at her! How many languages do you speak?

KATE MONSTER

Oh, come off it, Brian!
EVERYONE'S A LITTLE BIT RACIST.

BRIAN

I'm not!

PRINCETON

Oh no?

BRIAN

Nope!
HOW MANY ORIENTAL WIVES HAVE YOU GOT?

CHRISTMAS EVE

What? Brian!

PRINCETON

BRIAN, BUDDY, WHERE YOU BEEN?
THE TERM IS ASIAN AMERICAN!

CHRISTMAS EVE

I KNOW YOU ARE NO INTENDING TO BE,
BUT CALLING ME ORIENTAL—
OFFENSIVE TO ME!

BRIAN

I'm sorry, honey. I love you.

CHRISTMAS EVE

And I love you.

BRIAN

But you're racist too.

CHRISTMAS EVE

Yes, I know.

THE JEWS HAVE ALL THE MONEY
AND THE WHITES HAVE ALL THE POWER
AND I'M ALWAYS IN TAXI CAB WITH DRIVER WHO NO SHOWER!

PRINCETON

Me too!

KATE MONSTER

Me too!

GARY COLEMAN

I can't even get a taxi!

ALL

EVERYONE'S A LITTLE BIT RACIST—IT'S TRUE.
BUT EVERYONE IS JUST ABOUT AS RACIST—AS YOU!
IF WE ALL COULD JUST ADMIT
THAT WE ARE RACIST A LITTLE BIT
AND EVERYONE STOPPED BEING SO PC,
MAYBE
WE COULD
LIVE IN—HARMONY!

CHRISTMAS EVE

Ev'lyone's a ritter bit lacist!

(*Playoff.*)

SCENE 4A—CONTINUOUS

(PRINCETON *is alone.*)

PRINCETON

Today I feel like I'm getting closer to my purpose.

(*On the video screen, we see* PRINCETON *as a school crossing guard.*)

CHILDREN'S VOICES

School crossing guard!

PRINCETON

No—that's not me—

(*We see* PRINCETON *working at a nail salon, doing an old lady's nails.*)

CHILDREN'S VOICES

Manicurist!

PRINCETON

Not quite it.

(PRINCETON *as a clown.*)

CHILDREN'S VOICES

Birthday party clown!

PRINCETON

Closer—but still, no—
        (*A bell rings.*)
Wait a minute—I feel like it's right here, in the corner of my mind! My purpose! It's—it's—

(*Two adorable, snuggly bears appear.*)

BAD IDEA BEARS

Hey, Princeton!

GIRL BEAR

It's us!

PRINCETON

Who are you?

BAD IDEA BEARS

The Bad Idea Bears!

GIRL BEAR

We're your friends!

BOY BEAR

Where ya goin'?

PRINCETON

I'm almost broke. So I'm gonna get a job while I look for my purpose!

GIRL BEAR

Did the check come in from your folks?

PRINCETON

Yeah.

GIRL BEAR

Then you've got plenty of money!

BOY BEAR

You should celebrate!

GIRL BEAR

You need to do something for *you*. Buy some beer!

BOY BEAR

Yeah! Buy some beer!

PRINCETON

Gee, I shouldn't be spending my parents' money on beer.

BOY BEAR

(*Very sad.*)

Oh. Okay.

GIRL BEAR

That makes me sad, thinking about you not having any fun.

BOY BEAR

I'm gonna cry.

GIRL BEAR

(*Weeping.*)

Gosh, I'm sad. Some days, I wish I was dead.

PRINCETON

You know? Maybe I could afford a six-pack.

BAD IDEA BEARS

Yaaaaay!

GIRL BEAR

How 'bout a case!

BOY BEAR

A case of beer!

PRINCETON

Noo, no, I can't get a case.

GIRL BEAR

But you're on a budget!

BOY BEAR

You're wasting money in the long run if you don't buy in bulk!

PRINCETON

You're right. Wow, thanks, guys! I'll get a case.

BAD IDEA BEARS

Yaaaay!

BAD IDEA BEARS

See you around, Princeton!

(*They exit.*)

PRINCETON

See you around, guys! Gosh, they're awfully cute. It's good to know I'm making friends who have my best interests at heart.

SCENE 5—KATE'S APARTMENT / ON THE AVENUE

(*The phone rings twice. KATE answers.*)

KATE MONSTER

Hello?

(*A crabby old lady appears on the other end.*)

MRS. THISTLETWAT

Good morning, Katherine. This is your employer calling.

KATE MONSTER

Good morning, Mrs. Thistletwat!

MRS. THISTLETWAT

As you may know, I have an appointment for heart replacement surgery next week, and I need you to teach my class in the morning. I will probably need until the lunch break to recover.

KATE MONSTER

I get to teach all by myself?

MRS. THISTLETWAT

I trust you, Katherine. And you may choose the subject.

KATE MONSTER

Wow—thanks, Lavinia!

MRS. THISTLETWAT

Katherine, when you call me by my first name, the children don't respect me.

KATE MONSTER

Sorry, Mrs. Thistletwat.

MRS. THISTLETWAT

Thank you.

(*She disappears.*)

KATE MONSTER

(*To the audience.*)

Finally! I get to teach a whole lesson all by myself! And I'm gonna teach something relevant, something modern—the Internet!

(*Sings.*)

THE INTERNET IS REALLY, REALLY GREAT.

TREKKIE MONSTER

(*Appearing briefly.*)

FOR PORN!

KATE MONSTER

I GOT A FAST CONNECTION SO I DON'T HAVE TO WAIT.

TREKKIE MONSTER

(*Appearing again.*)

FOR PORN!

KATE MONSTER

THERE'S ALWAYS SOME NEW SITE.

TREKKIE MONSTER

FOR PORN!

KATE MONSTER

I BROWSE ALL DAY AND NIGHT.

TREKKIE MONSTER

FOR PORN!

KATE MONSTER

IT'S LIKE I'M SURFING AT THE SPEED OF LIGHT.

TREKKIE MONSTER

FOR PORN!

KATE MONSTER

Trekkie!

TREKKIE	**KATE**
THE INTERNET IS FOR PORN!	Trekkie!
THE INTERNET IS FOR PORN!	What are you doing?
WHY YOU THINK THE NET WAS	
BORN?	
PORN! PORN! PORN!	

KATE MONSTER

Trekkie Monster!!

TREKKIE MONSTER

Wha—wha?

KATE MONSTER

Get down here!

TREKKIE MONSTER

Yeah, yeah.

 (TREKKIE *appears next to* KATE.)

Hello, Kate Monster.

KATE MONSTER

You are ruining my song.

TREKKIE MONSTER

Oh, me sorry. Me no mean to.

KATE MONSTER

Well, if you wouldn't mind, please, being quiet for a minute so I can finish?

TREKKIE MONSTER

Okey-dokey.

KATE MONSTER

Good.
(*Sings.*)
I'M GLAD WE HAVE THIS NEW TECHNOLOGY.

TREKKIE MONSTER

FOR PORN. (OOOPS.)

KATE MONSTER

WHICH GIVES US UNTOLD OPPORTUNITY.

TREKKIE MONSTER

FOR PORN. (OOOPS, SORRY.)

KATE MONSTER

RIGHT FROM YOUR OWN DESKTOP—

TREKKIE MONSTER

FOR P—.

KATE MONSTER

YOU CAN RESEARCH, BROWSE, AND SHOP—

TREKKIE MONSTER

—.

KATE MONSTER

UNTIL YOU'VE HAD ENOUGH AND YOU'RE READY TO STOP!

TREKKIE MONSTER

FOR PORN!

KATE MONSTER

Trekkie!

TREKKIE		**KATE**
THE INTERNET IS FOR PORN!	Trekkie!	
THE INTERNET IS FOR PORN!	HMMM!	
ME UP ALL NIGHT HONKING ME		
HORN TO		
PORN, PORN, PORN!		

KATE MONSTER

That's gross! You're a pervert!

TREKKIE MONSTER

Ah, sticks and stones, Kate Monster.

KATE MONSTER

No, really, you're a pervert! *Normal* people don't sit at home and look at porn on the Internet!

(TREKKIE MONSTER *gives a long look to the audience, then looks back at* KATE MONSTER.)

KATE MONSTER

What?

TREKKIE MONSTER

You have no idea. Ready, normal people?

(ROD, BRIAN, PRINCETON, *and* GARY *appear.*)

BRIAN

Ready!

GARY COLEMAN

Ready!

ROD

Ready!

TREKKIE MONSTER

Lemme hear it!

GUYS

THE INTERNET IS FOR PORN!

PRINCETON

Sorry, Kate!

GUYS

THE INTERNET IS FOR PORN!

PRINCETON

I masturbate!

TREKKIE MONSTER

ALL THESE GUYS UNZIP THEIR FLIES FOR

GUYS	**KATE**
PORN! PORN! PORN! POOORN, POORN—	The Internet is *not* for porn!

KATE MONSTER

Hold on a second!

TREKKIE MONSTER

Wha?

KATE MONSTER

Now, I happen to know for a fact that you, Rod, check your portfolio and trade stocks online.

ROD

That's correct.

KATE MONSTER

And, Brian, you buy things on Amazon.com!

BRIAN

Sure.

KATE MONSTER

And, Gary, you keep selling your possessions on eBay!

GARY COLEMAN

Yes, I do.

KATE MONSTER

And, Princeton, you sent me that sweet online birthday card.

PRINCETON

True.

TREKKIE MONSTER

But, Kate . . . what you think he do *after,* hmmm?

(PRINCETON *nods, guiltily.*)

KATE MONSTER

Ewww!

GUYS	KATE
THE INTERNET IS FOR PORN!	Gross!
THE INTERNET IS FOR PORN!	I hate porn!
GRAB YOUR DICK AND DOUBLE CLICK FOR	Ohhh!
PORN! PORN! PORN!	I hate men!
POOORN!	I'm leaving!
POOORN!	I hate the Internet!
THE INTERNET IS FOR	
INTERNET IS FOR	
INTERNET IS FOR	
PORN!	

SCENE 6— ON THE AVENUE

(CHRISTMAS EVE *and* ROD.)

CHRISTMAS EVE

Hey, Rod, how it hanging?

ROD

Christmas Eve, I got your wedding invitation!

CHRISTMAS EVE

Are you coming?

ROD

Here's my RSVP!

(*He hands her an envelope.* BRIAN *appears in a window, holding an invitation.*)

BRIAN

Hey, honey? What's all this about us getting married?

CHRISTMAS EVE

Think of it like a surprise party.

BRIAN

Cool!

(*He closes the window.*)

ROD

(*A bit sad.*)

I think it's wonderful that you have someone so special in your life.

CHRISTMAS EVE

Are you okay, Rod?

ROD

Christmas Eve, you're a therapist, right?

CHRISTMAS EVE

I have two master degree!

ROD

So you help people who have all kinds of problems?

CHRISTMAS EVE

Nobody want to come to me for helping. I meet with people, we talking for an hour, then they go away and never come back. And I wonder: why? Am I fixing them in one appointment? Maybe I too efficient. Maybe I should spread my helping out! Why, Rod, do you need some helping?

ROD

Well—I have this friend—

CHRISTMAS EVE

Nicky?

ROD

No, no—another friend. And I think he has a very big problem. I think—I think my friend is
(*Whispers.*)
gay.

CHRISTMAS EVE

What wrong with that? You know, Rod, gay people make major contribution to art and philosophy and literature for many hundreds of years now.

ROD

But my friend isn't an artist—he's a Republican. And an investment banker.

CHRISTMAS EVE

Ew, well, tell him to stay in closet then. He good for nothing.

ROD

(*A moment.*)
Well, okay! Great! Thanks for the advice!

CHRISTMAS EVE

Yeah, I wouldn't want a friend like that.

ROD

Thanks again!

CHRISTMAS EVE

Bye now.

(*She goes inside.*)

ROD

Bye-bye!
(*Beat. To the audience.*)
Shit.

SCENE 7—KATE'S APARTMENT

(KATE *is by herself.*)

KATE MONSTER

Princeton.
(*Singing.*)
HE LIKES ME.
I THINK HE LIKES ME.
BUT DOES HE LIKE ME LIKE ME
LIKE I LIKE HIM?
WILL WE BE FRIENDS
OR SOMETHING MORE?
I THINK HE'S INTERESTED
BUT I'M NOT SURE.

(*Doorbell.*)

KATE MONSTER

Come in!

(PRINCETON *enters.*)

PRINCETON

Hiya, Kate!

KATE MONSTER

Princeton! Hi!

PRINCETON

Listen, I was going through my old CDs yesterday, and I kept coming across songs I thought you'd like, so I made you this mix.

KATE MONSTER

Oh, that's so sweet! Can I get you a drink? Or a snack?

PRINCETON

Actually, do you mind if I use your bathroom?

KATE MONSTER

Go right ahead.

PRINCETON

Thank you!

KATE MONSTER

A MIX TAPE.
HE MADE A MIX TAPE.
HE WAS THINKING OF ME
WHICH SHOWS HE CARES!
SOMETIMES WHEN SOMEONE
HAS A CRUSH ON YOU
THEY'LL MAKE YOU A MIX TAPE
TO GIVE YOU A CLUE.
Let's see . . .
"YOU'VE GOT A FRIEND"
"THE THEME FROM FRIENDS"
"THAT'S WHAT FRIENDS ARE FOR"
Shit.

Oh, but look!
"A WHOLE NEW WORLD"
"KISS THE GIRL"
"MY CHERIE AMOUR"
Awww, Princeton! He does like me!

"I AM THE WALRUS"
"FAT BOTTOM GIRLS"
"YELLOW SUBMARINE"
WHAT DOES THIS MEAN?

(PRINCETON *re-enters.*)

PRINCETON
Hey, Kate, you might wanna not go in there for a while.

KATE MONSTER
Princeton, thank you for the mix. I was just looking at disc one. Great songs!

PRINCETON
Did you get to disc two yet?

KATE MONSTER
Not yet.

PRINCETON
Oh, it's great. Check it out.

KATE MONSTER
"STUCK ON YOU"

PRINCETON
"LOVE ME DO"

KATE MONSTER
"MY HEART WILL GO ON"
I loved *Titanic*!

PRINCETON

It was all right.
"SHE'S GOT A WAY"

KATE MONSTER

"YESTERDAY"

PRINCETON

"GOODNIGHT SAIGON"
From the Russia concert!

KATE MONSTER

Don't know that one.
"THROUGH THE YEARS"

PRINCETON

"THE THEME FROM CHEERS"

KATE MONSTER

"MOVING RIGHT ALONG"
Nice mix.

PRINCETON

There's one more . . .
"I HAVE TO SAY I LOVE YOU IN A SONG"

KATE MONSTER

Princeton, that's so sweet! I've never gotten such a nice present from a guy.

PRINCETON

Awww. I'm glad you like it. But I have to go now. I'm gonna make one for Brian and Christmas Eve, and Gary, and Nicky and Rod, and Trekkie Monster, and everyone!

KATE MONSTER

Umm.

PRINCETON

And oh—

KATE MONSTER

Yes?

PRINCETON

What are you doing tonight?

KATE MONSTER

Grading term papers. But it's kindergarten so they're very short. Why?

PRINCETON

Everyone's going to hear this singer at the Around the Clock Cafe. Do you want to go with me?

KATE MONSTER

Like, a date?

PRINCETON

Sure! A date. It'll be a blast.

KATE MONSTER

I'd love to come!

PRINCETON

Well, I'll see you then.

KATE MONSTER

Okay!

PRINCETON

Okay, bye.

KATE MONSTER

Bye!

PRINCETON

Bye!

(*He exits.*)

KATE MONSTER

He likes me!

SCENE 8—AROUND THE CLOCK CAFÉ

(*At a homey café.*)

BRIAN

(*Offstage.*)
Ladies and gentlemen, I now present the comic stylings of the funniest person I know—me!

(*He rushes onstage and sings.*)
I'M NOT WEARING UNDERWEAR TODAY
NO, I'M NOT WEARING UNDERWEAR TODAY
NOT THAT YOU PROB'LY CARE

MUCH ABOUT MY UNDERWEAR
STILL NONETHELESS I GOTTA SAY
THAT I'M NOT WEARING UNDERWEAR TO-DAAAAY!

(*Big finish. Nobody claps.*)

CHRISTMAS EVE

Get a job!

BRIAN

Thank you—honey. But don't move a muscle, ladies and gentlemen!
We'll be right back with our headline performer!

(TREKKIE MONSTER *and* GARY *are sitting on a bench.*)

GARY COLEMAN

Say, Trekkie, you never leave your apartment. What made you drag your
furry ass out here?

TREKKIE MONSTER

Me see pictures of next singer on Internet.

(*He shivers with desire.*)

(KATE MONSTER *and* PRINCETON *enter, dressed nicely.*)

PRINCETON

There's an empty table!

KATE MONSTER

Let's grab it!

PRINCETON

Ladies first!

KATE MONSTER

Oh! Princeton, you're such a gentleman!

PRINCETON

You too. I mean, you look like a knockout tonight.

KATE MONSTER

(*Giggling.*)

You!

(*They sit.* BRIAN *takes the stage.*)

BRIAN

So—here's the woman you all came to see—
(*Reading from an index card.*)
"The Around the Clock is proud to present—fresh from her world tour, headlining in Amsterdam, Bangkok, and Celebration, Florida—please give a warm hand to the star of *Girls Gone Wild* parts two, five, and seven—Lucy the Slut!"

(*Dramatic lighting onstage.* LUCY *appears. She's a knockout.*)

LUCY

I CAN MAKE YOU FEEL
SPECIAL
WHEN IT SUCKS TO BE YOU.
LET ME MAKE YOU FEEL
SPECIAL
FOR AN HOUR OR TWO.

YOUR LIFE'S A ROUTINE THAT REPEATS EACH DAY.
NO ONE CARES WHO YOU ARE OR WHAT YOU SAY.
AND SOMETIMES YOU FEEL LIKE YOU'RE NOBODY
BUT YOU CAN FEEL LIKE SOMEBODY
WITH ME!

PRINCETON

Wow!

(LUCY *has a dance break and dazzles the guys with her sexiness.*)

LUCY

Yeah, they're real.
(*Her dance continues.*)
WHEN WE'RE TOGETHER THE EARTH WILL SHAKE
AND THE STARS WILL FALL INTO THE SEA!
SO COME ON, BABY
LET DOWN YOUR GUARD.
WHEN YOUR DATE'S IN THE BATHROOM I'LL SLIP YOU MY CARD!
I CAN TELL JUST BY LOOKING THAT YOU'VE GOT IT HARD
FOR ME! FOR ME!
FOR ME! FOR ME! FOR ME! FOR ME!
I CAN TELL JUST BY LOOKING THAT YOU ARE ESPECIALLY HARD
FOR ME!
(*Music ends. The crowd applauds.*)
Thank you, gentlemen and obstacles to those gentlemen. Have a few
drinks, and I sure hope you enjoyed my set.

(*She leaves the stage.* TREKKIE *tries to follow her.* BRIAN *stops
him.*)

BRIAN

No, Trekkie.

TREKKIE MONSTER

Oh, but, Brian!

BRIAN

No!

TREKKIE MONSTER

Me need to hurry home—*now!*

(*He rushes offstage. At* PRINCETON *and* KATE*'s table.*)

PRINCETON

Wow, that Lucy's something, isn't she?

KATE MONSTER

She's something.

PRINCETON

Can I get you a drink, Kate?

KATE MONSTER

I'll get a water. I gotta be chipper to teach tomorrow! It's a big day! The teacher I'm assisting is going into the hospital tomorrow morning. So I have the entire class to myself! And if I do well, it could mean a big career boost!

(*The* BAD IDEA BEARS *pop up behind* KATE *and* PRINCETON. *They hold two giant drinks.*)

BAD IDEA BEARS

Hey, guys!

BOY BEAR

We brought you some Long Island Iced Teas!

KATE MONSTER

Ohhh, you're so adorable! Who are you?

GIRL BEAR

We're your friends! Have a drink, Kate!

KATE MONSTER

Ohhh, no, thank you.

BOY BEAR

Just a little, ittle sip!

KATE MONSTER

I really shouldn't—

BOY BEAR

But it's only a Long Island Iced Tea!

GIRL BEAR

They're so sweet and delicious!

BOY BEAR

Please?

GIRL BEAR

Please?

KATE MONSTER

(*Cheerfully.*)

Well, one sip can't hurt. Cheers, Princeton!

PRINCETON

Cheers! Here's to you, Kate Monster!

(KATE *and* PRINCETON *sip their drinks through straws.*)

BAD IDEA BEARS

Yaaaay!

KATE MONSTER

That's delicious!

BOY BEAR

Why don't you play a drinking game?

GIRL BEAR

What a neat idea!

BOY BEAR

That's a recipe for fun!

KATE MONSTER

I don't know any drinking games. Do you, Princeton?

GIRL BEAR

I know one! It's called "I bet I can drink faster than you can!"

BAD IDEA BEARS

One—two—three—

KATE MONSTER

But—

BAD IDEA BEARS

Go!

(KATE *and* PRINCETON *drain their drinks to the bottom.*)

Yaaaaay!

BOY BEAR

It was a tie!

GIRL BEAR

Rematch!

KATE MONSTER

Gosh, that's nummy!

BAD IDEA BEARS

Another round!

KATE MONSTER

I'll get the next one, Princeton.

PRINCETON

Great!

KATE MONSTER

I'll be back in a sec!

GIRL BEAR

But this time, Kate, let's get larges!

KATE MONSTER

(*A little drunk.*)
Oooooh-kay!

BOY BEAR

Hey, how's the date going, huh?

PRINCETON

Pretty well, I think—

BOY BEAR

Now just hang in there, little man, you're gonna get her muffin if you just keep working at it! Keep your eye on the prize! Oh, wow! Look who's coming!

(LUCY *comes over.*)

LUCY

What's up.

PRINCETON

Hi, I'm Princeton.

LUCY

Lucy. Man, am I beat. I still haven't figured out where I'm gonna crash tonight.

BOY BEAR

Feel her boob!

PRINCETON

Shhhh!

(KATE *enters. She stops when she sees* LUCY *with* PRINCETON.)

LUCY

All I need is a warm mattress, you know?

PRINCETON

Mine's pretty cold, usually.

LUCY

It wouldn't be cold for long. Where's your pad?

KATE MONSTER

(*Rushing over.*)
The drinks will be right over, Princeton!
(*To* LUCY.)
Oh, why, hel-lo!

LUCY

I'll have a scotch on the rocks.

KATE MONSTER

I'm not a waitress.

PRINCETON

Lucy, I'd like you to meet Kate Monster.

LUCY

Oh, you're dating a Monster. I dated a Monster once. But I got sick of
picking the fur out of my teeth.

KATE MONSTER

If your teeth are the problem, I could take out a couple.

The full original Broadway cast of *Avenue Q*. (Photo © Carol Rosegg)

Left to right, bottom to top: Stephanie D'Abruzzo, Jennifer Barnhart, Princeton, and John Tartaglia in the Broadway production. (Photo © Carol Rosegg)

Left to right: Rod, John Tartaglia, Nicky, Jennifer Barnhart, and Rick Lyon in the Broadway production. (Photo © Carol Rosegg)

Kate Monster and Stephanie D'Abruzzo in the Broadway production. (Photo ©
Carol Rosegg)

Rod and John Tartaglia in the Broadway production. (Photo © Carol Rosegg)

Jennifer Barnhart, Trekkie Monster, and Rick Lyon in the Broadway production. (Photo © Carol Rosegg)

Princeton, John Tartaglia, Kate Monster, and Brynn O'Malley in the Las Vegas production. (Photo © Carol Rosegg)

Lucy the Slut and Sarah Stiles in the Broadway production. (Photo © Carol Rosegg)

PRINCETON

(*Breaking them up.*)
Hey—it was nice talking to you, Lucy!

LUCY

Have fun with your Monster. But when you're ready for a real woman, you know where to find me.

(LUCY *leaves.*)

PRINCETON

Oh man, Kate, I'm sorry.

KATE MONSTER

No, I understand.
(*Flirting.*)
You're irresistible, is all.

PRINCETON

Aw. Well, she just knows she can't compare to you.

KATE MONSTER

I think you're wonderful, Princeton.

(*A moment as their eyes meet, and they shyly look away. The* BEARS *creep up and whisper to* PRINCETON.)

BOY BEAR

Take her home!

GIRL BEAR

She's wasted!

PRINCETON

Would you guys cut that out?

> (*To* KATE.)

Kate—

KATE MONSTER

Hmmmm?

PRINCETON

I think you look really beautiful tonight.

KATE MONSTER

Oh, Princeton, you look so handsome I could eat you alive!

> (*They begin to mash.*)

BAD IDEA BEARS

More drinks! More fun! Yaaaaay!

SCENE 9—KATE'S APARTMENT / ENTIRE STREET

> (*In* KATE's *bedroom, the covers are writhing.* KATE *and* PRINCETON *are going at it, moaning in pleasure.*)

KATE MONSTER

My God, Princeton! Right there! Right there! That's the spot—that's the—no, a little lower—now to the left—no, my left—Ohhhhhhhh!

> (*More writhing.*)

PRINCETON

Kate, no one's ever touched me like—you can't put your finger there—I mean *put your finger there*—Ahhhhhh!

(They dive under the covers, screaming in pleasure.)

KATE MONSTER

Aaaaahhh!

PRINCETON

Yaaaaahhh!

(Lights up on GARY COLEMAN, *who's listening in.)*

GARY COLEMAN

(Sings.)
YOU CAN BE AS LOUD AS THE HELL YOU WANT
WHEN YOU'RE MAKING LOVE!

(The BAD IDEA BEARS *pop up.)*

BEARS

WHEN YOU'RE MAKING LOVE!

GARY COLEMAN

YOU CAN BE AS LOUD AS THE HELL YOU WANT
WHEN YOU'RE MAKING LOVE!

BEARS

WHEN YOU'RE MAKING LOVE!

GARY COLEMAN

YOU CAN BE AS LOUD AS THE HELL YOU WANT

WHEN YOU'RE MAKING LOVE!

BEARS

WHEN YOU'RE MAKING LOVE!

GARY AND BEARS

YOU CAN BE AS LOUD AS THE HELL YOU WANT!

(*A flowerpot is thrown from an unseen window, nearly hitting* GARY. *A complaining voice shouts, "Shut the fuck up!"*)

(*Lights up on* PRINCETON *and* KATE, *who pop up from under the covers.*)

KATE MONSTER

Are we being too loud?

PRINCETON

Yeah, are we bothering someone?

GARY COLEMAN

Not at all, kids. You keep doing what you're doing.

GIRL BEAR

Yeah!

BAD IDEA BEARS

Louder!

GARY COLEMAN

YOU'RE NOT ALLOWED TO BE LOUD AT A LIBRARY
AT THE ART MUSEUM OR AT A PLAY—

BAD IDEA BEARS

AT A PLAY—

GARY COLEMAN

BUT WHEN YOU AND YOUR PARTNER
ARE DOIN' THE NASTY

ALL

DON'T BEHAVE LIKE YOU'RE AT THE BALLET!

GARY COLEMAN

'CUZ YOU CAN BE AS LOUD AS THE HELL YOU WANT
WHEN YOU'RE MAKING LOVE!

BAD IDEA BEARS

MAKING SWEET, SWEET LOVE!

GARY COLEMAN

YEAH! YOU CAN BE AS LOUD AS THE HELL YOU WANT
WHEN YOU'RE MAKING LOVE!

BAD IDEA BEARS

LOUD AS THE HELL! LOUD AS THE HELL!

GARY COLEMAN

DON'T LET YO' NEIGHBORS STOP YOU FROM HAVIN' FUN.
THEY'LL HAVE PEACE AND QUIET WHEN YOU'RE GOOD AND DONE.

ALL

BE AS LOUD AS THE HELL YOU WANT WHEN YOU'RE MAKING LOVE!
    (*Heavy breathing.*)
LOUD AS THE HELL YOU WANT—

KATE MONSTER

Faster, Princeton!

CHRISTMAS EVE

Brian, slow down! This not a race!

ALL

LOUD AS THE HELL YOU WANT—

PRINCETON

Oh *yeah*!

BRIAN

Who's your daddy?

CHRISTMAS EVE

What? Brian!

ALL

LOUD AS THE HELL YOU WANT!
LOUD AS THE HELL YOU WANT!

GARY COLEMAN

Smack it and lick it and rub it and suck it!

ALL

LOUD AS THE HELL YOU WANT!

CHRISTMAS EVE

Yes! Work your mama!

ALL

LOUD AS THE HELL YOU—

KATE MONSTER

Oh yeah, that's it!

BRIAN

Ohh, babe!

PRINCETON

Holy cow!

(TREKKIE *appears, pleasuring himself.*)

TREKKIE

UUUUUUHHH!

ALL

LOUD AS THE HELL YOU
LOUD AS THE HELL YOU
LOUD AS THE HELL YOU
LOUD AS THE HELL YOU
LOUD AS THE HELL YOU
LOUD AS THE HELL YOU
LOUD AS THE HELL YOU
LOUD AS THE HELL YOU
LOUD AS THE HELL YOU—
WANT!

(*A video. Two heads, on the left a male and on the right a female, exchange the word "commitment." The male says "come" in an increasingly fevered manner, while the female says "mitment" in a more annoyed tone. At the end, they both say: "Commitment!"*)

SCENE 10—NICKY AND ROD'S APARTMENT / KATE'S APARTMENT

(ROD *is awake in bed while* NICKY *snores.*)

ROD

It sure can get lonely at night. Nicky, are you awake?

NICKY

(*Asleep.*)
Is that a unicorn?

ROD

Oh no, he's talking in his sleep again.

NICKY

I can put on the purple shoes. Who painted the kitten?

ROD

Maybe I should shake him.

NICKY

I love you, Rod.

ROD

What did you say?

NICKY

I love your little laugh.

ROD

Nicky, are you awake?

NICKY

Take off your shirt.

ROD

Oh, Nicholas. Have we been hiding from each other all this time? I wonder.

(*Sings.*)
ALL THOSE NIGHTS I LAY IN BED
THOUGHTS OF YOU RUNNING THROUGH MY HEAD—

NICKY

Who put my earmuffs on the cookie?

ROD

BUT I NEVER THOUGHT THE THINGS IN MY HEAD
COULD REALLY HAPPEN IN MY BED.

NICKY

You look like David Hasselhoff.

ROD

ALL THOSE YEARS I MISSED THE SIGNS
COULDN'T READ BETWEEN THE LINES—
WHO'D HAVE THOUGHT I WOULD SEE THE DAY
WHERE I'D HEAR YOU SAY WHAT I HEARD YOU SAY?
AND NOW I FIND WHAT WAS ALWAYS IN MY MIND
WAS IN YOUR MIND TOO.
WHO KNEW?!
FANTASIES COME TRUE!
AND NOW I SEE
THAT WHAT I'VE ALWAYS DREAMED OF WAS MEANT TO BE—
YOU AND ME,

ME AND YOU—
FANTASIES COME TRUE!
> (*Onstage, a fantasy sequence unfolds with* ROD *and* NICKY
> *running into each others' arms,* NICKY *dipping a joyous* ROD.)

YOU AND ME
LIVED IN FANTASY
BUT SOON WE'LL BE A REALITY.

> (*We cut to* KATE *and* PRINCETON, *who are in bed.*)

PRINCETON

Kate, that was amazing.

KATE MONSTER

You're amazing.

PRINCETON

Listen—I want you to have this. It's a penny I carry around with me for good luck. It's from the year I was born—see? Who knows, maybe it'll bring you good luck. It did for me! I found you.
> (*Sings.*)

I WANT YOU TO KNOW
THE TIME THAT WE'VE SPENT
HOW GREAT IT'S BEEN
HOW MUCH IT'S MEANT.

KATE MONSTER

GOSH, I DON'T KNOW WHAT TO SAY.
I'M REALLY GLAD YOU FEEL THAT WAY.
'CUZ I'M AFRAID THAT I LIKE YOU MORE
THAN I'VE EVER LIKED ANY GUY BEFORE!

ROD AND KATE

'CUZ NOW, MY LOVE,
I'M GETTING WHAT I'VE ALWAYS BEEN DREAMING OF.
SO ARE YOU.

KATE MONSTER

OH, BABY.

ROD AND KATE

FANTASIES COME TRUE!
AND NOW I SWEAR THAT WHEN YOU WANT ME,
I'M GONNA BE RIGHT THERE
TO CARE FOR YOU—

KATE MONSTER

THAT'S WHAT I'M GONNA DO.

ROD AND KATE

AND MAKE YOUR FANTASIES COME TRUE!

ROD

FANTASIES COME TRUE.

(ROD *awakens.* NICKY *is poking him.*)

NICKY

Hey, Rod buddy! You were talking in your sleep.

ROD

I thought you were talking in *your* sleep!

NICKY

No, I just came to bed. You were dreaming, is all.

ROD

Oh.

NICKY

It sounded like a nice dream, though.

ROD

Yes. It was a nice dream.

NICKY

Good night.

ROD

Good night, Nicky.

(*He looks at* NICKY *wistfully.*)

SCENE 11—KATE'S APARTMENT

(*Daylight.* KATE *and* PRINCETON *are in bed. The phone rings, and* KATE *picks it up sleepily.*)

KATE MONSTER

Hello?

(MRS. THISTLETWAT *appears.*)

MRS. THISTLETWAT

Good afternoon, Katherine. You may recall that you were supposed to teach my class this morning—*while I got my heart replaced!*

KATE MONSTER

Oh my God!

MRS. THISTLETWAT

You left the children unattended for three hours! They created their own tribal society, and were about to sacrifice poor little Brittany! Where were you?!

KATE MONSTER

I—I overslept—I'm so sorry—

MRS. THISTLETWAT

I should have never hired a Monster!

KATE MONSTER

What?

MRS. THISTLETWAT

Your race is notoriously lazy.

KATE MONSTER

Well, better a Monster than a crabby old bitch!

(KATE *and* MRS. THISTLETWAT *gasp in unison,* KATE *shocked at herself.*)

MRS. THISTLETWAT

Crabby old bitches are the bedrock of this nation! I regret the day I hired you!

KATE MONSTER

That's okay, because I quit!

MRS. THISTLETWAT

No, I'm going to fire you!

KATE MONSTER

But you can't fire me, because I quit!

MRS. THISTLETWAT

You're going to hell, Katherine!

KATE MONSTER

See ya there!

(*She hangs up and* MRS. THISTLETWAT *vanishes. A moment.*)

Was I too mean?

PRINCETON

Good for you!

KATE MONSTER

I hated working for her! I can get by on my savings for a while, and temp a little bit, and pursue what I really want in my life!

PRINCETON

Your school!

KATE MONSTER

Yes!

PRINCETON

I think you're really brave, Kate.

KATE MONSTER

Yeah?

(*A moment. They look at each other, then away shyly.*)

PRINCETON

Listen, are you going to Brian and Christmas Eve's wedding?

KATE MONSTER

Of course!

PRINCETON

I was thinking maybe we could go, you know, together.

KATE MONSTER

Oh my gosh—it seems like I always go to weddings alone. I don't know what I'd *do* if I went with—

(*A moment.*)

PRINCETON

With a boyfriend?

KATE MONSTER

Yeah—

(*A moment.*)

PRINCETON

Then come with me.

KATE MONSTER

(*Emotionally.*)
That'd be great!

PRINCETON

Are you okay, Kate?

KATE MONSTER

Yeah, yeah. I just get fur in my eyes sometimes.

(*He pulls her toward him, and they kiss.*)

SCENE 12—THE WEDDING

(*The street is decorated festively.* GARY *stands at the top of the stoop, dressed sharply, with a book.*)

(*The wedding march plays.* ROD *and* NICKY *enter, dressed in tuxedos.*)

ROD

(*To* NICKY.)
Did you get the camera?

NICKY

Camera?

ROD

The one I left on the bed—it was on the bed—

(*He snaps away.* KATE *and* PRINCETON *enter, dressed formally.*)

PRINCETON

You look beautiful, Kate.

KATE MONSTER

Thank you.

(BRIAN *enters nervously in a tux.* CHRISTMAS EVE *enters in an over-the-top wedding dress.*)

GARY COLEMAN

And by the power vested in me as a former child celebrity, I now pronounce you husband and wife.

(BRIAN *steps on a glass.*)

CHRISTMAS EVE

L'chaim!

EVERYONE

Mazel tov!

(CHRISTMAS EVE *and* BRIAN *kiss. Party music begins.* NICKY *approaches* ROD.)

NICKY

That sure was beautiful, wasn't it, Rod?

ROD

They're so lucky to have each other. Gee.

NICKY

Are you upset, Rod?

ROD

Nicky, I need a moment by myself.

NICKY

No, buddy, talk to me. What's the matter?

(*In another part of the stage.*)

BRIAN

Hey, what's up with Rod?

GARY COLEMAN

Yeah, he's sure lookin' down in the dumps lately.

CHRISTMAS EVE

He lonely. He need a girlfriend.

GARY COLEMAN

A girlfriend? You gotta be kidding! Rod?

CHRISTMAS EVE

He not so ugly.

GARY COLEMAN

But I always figured Rod was one of those gays!

CHRISTMAS EVE

Rod? Is gay?

BRIAN

I bet Nicky would know. Hey, Nicky, come over here.

(NICKY *comes over, leaving* ROD *alone.*)

NICKY

Sure, guys.

CHRISTMAS EVE

(*Stage whisper.*)

We wondering if Rod is a gay.

NICKY

It's funny you ask. Because I do think Rod is gay. I always have. But I figured if he wanted to tell me, he would. So yes, definitely, I would say that my buddy Rod is a closeted homosexual.

ROD

(*Overhearing, gasps.*)

Nicky! How could you say that about me?

NICKY

(*He freezes.*)

Oh, hi, Rod. All I said was, "Yes, definitely, I would say that my buddy Rod has an undescended testicle."

(*The group agrees.*)

ROD

No, I heard you!

NICKY

Gee, I'm sorry, Rod.

ROD

Well, I'm *not* a closeted homowhatever! I have a whole life that none of you know about! Not even you, Nicky!

NICKY

You do, Rod?

ROD

Sure I do! For example—I . . . I . . .

(He suddenly bursts out in song.)

OHHHHHHHHHHHHH . . .

I WISH YOU COULD MEET MY GIRLFRIEND,

MY GIRLFRIEND, WHO LIVES IN CANADA.

SHE COULDN'T BE SWEETER,

I WISH YOU COULD MEET HER,

MY GIRLFRIEND, WHO LIVES IN CANADA!

HER NAME IS ALBERTA,

SHE LIVES IN VANCOUVER.

SHE COOKS LIKE MY MOTHER

AND SUCKS LIKE A HOOVER.

I E-MAIL HER EVERY SINGLE DAY

JUST TO MAKE SURE THAT EVERYTHING'S OKAY.

IT'S A PITY SHE LIVES SO FAR AWAY,

IN CANADA!

LAAAAST

WEEK SHE WAS HERE BUT SHE HAD THE FLU.

TOO BAAAAAD

'CAUSE I WANTED TO INTRODUCE HER TO YOU.

IT'S SO SAAAAAAAAD

THERE WASN'T A THING THAT SHE COULD DO

BUT STAY IN BED

WITH HER LEGS UP OVER HER HEAD!

OH!

I WISH YOU COULD MEET MY GIRLFRIEND

BUT YOU CAN'T, BECAUSE SHE IS IN CANADA.

I LOVE HER, I MISS HER

I CAN'T WAIT TO KISS HER
SO SOON I'LL BE OFF TO ALBERTA!
I MEAN VANCOUVER!
SHIT! HER NAME IS ALBERTA,
SHE LIVES IN VANCOU—

SHE'S MY GIRLFRIEND!
MY WONDERFUL GIRLFRIEND!
YES, I HAVE A GIRLFRIEND,
WHO LIVES IN CANADA!
    (*Speaks.*)
And I can't wait to eat her pussy again!

    (*A long moment.*)

    (*Everyone shifts uncomfortably.*)

GARY COLEMAN

My goodness, would you look at the time! I really should get movin'. Yes sir.

CHRISTMAS EVE

    (*Uncomfortably, to* BRIAN.)
Maybe we go to buffet—

BRIAN

Yeah, I'm starving—

KATE MONSTER

We'll join you—

    (*They exit, leaving* NICKY *with* ROD.)

NICKY

Rod, all I meant was: I'd still be your buddy even if you were gay!

ROD

(*Quietly.*)

Nicky, I want you out of the apartment when I get back.

NICKY

You're kicking me out?

ROD

Go live in a garbage can for all I care!

(ROD *exits.*)

NICKY

But, Rod—Oh, gee. I'd better see if I can patch things up with Rod.

(*Exiting.*)

I didn't make him mad on purpose.

(PRINCETON *enters on "purpose."*)

(*A bell rings and* PRINCETON*'s head snaps up.*)

PRINCETON

Purpose.

CHRISTMAS EVE

(*To* KATE.)

I throw bouquet in few minutes, Kate Monster. I have eye on good husband for you!

KATE MONSTER

(*Blushing.*)
Christmas Eve!

CHRISTMAS EVE

I might throw bouquet to you on purpose!

(*She exits with* BRIAN. *Another bell rings.*)

PRINCETON

Purpose.

KATE MONSTER

Oh, Princeton, I have so much fun with you.

PRINCETON

Me too!

KATE MONSTER

What are you doing tomorrow?

PRINCETON

Gosh, it seems like I'm forgetting something.

KATE MONSTER

(*Looks off.*)
Oh, she's throwing the bouquet! I'll be right back.

PRINCETON

(*Thinking.*)
Purpose. Huh. Purpose?

(*The word "PURPOSE" appears on the video screen. The "U" and "R" switch, and the "U" becomes an "O," and it suddenly reads "PROPOSE." Dramatic sting. The word becomes nightmarish, and lights swirl around a dizzy* PRINCETON, *who begins to hallucinate:* BRIAN *and* CHRISTMAS EVE *at the altar, but with the faces of* PRINCETON *and* KATE; *a giant* KATE MONSTER *towering over the entire neighborhood, with a bouquet.*)

(*Suddenly, the nightmare stops, and* KATE *stands by* PRINCETON. *They are alone. She holds a bouquet.*)

KATE MONSTER
I caught the bouquet, Princeton! Well, some little girl caught it, but she wasn't very strong.

PRINCETON
Yeah.

(*A moment.*)

KATE MONSTER
Are you all right?

PRINCETON
Kate—I have something I need to say.

KATE MONSTER
Princeton, you can tell me anything.

PRINCETON
Listen, when I moved here to Avenue Q, I was looking for my purpose.

KATE MONSTER

I remember.

PRINCETON

And we've been spending so much time together—and I've lost track of finding it.

KATE MONSTER

Uh-huh.

PRINCETON

I don't want to be an old man and look back and realize I never found my reason to be alive.

   (*A moment.*)

KATE MONSTER

So—hm.

PRINCETON

Yeah.

KATE MONSTER

So—you don't want to spend time with me anymore?

PRINCETON

No! I love being with you.

KATE MONSTER

Oh, good, because I thought you meant—

PRINCETON

But I don't want a girlfriend until I figure out my mission in life!

(*A moment.*)

KATE MONSTER

But you—

PRINCETON

Kate, if we stay together, believe me, we'll never even be friends in the end.

KATE MONSTER

But I'm not looking for friends. I have plenty of friends.

PRINCETON

But you like me, don't you?

KATE MONSTER

Well—yes. I do. And I think that's why you should get out of here.

PRINCETON

You mean I should leave?

KATE MONSTER

Unless you have another definition for "get out of here."
(PRINCETON *waits uncertainly, then exits.*)
(KATE *is alone.*)
THERE'S A FINE, FINE LINE
BETWEEN A LOVER AND A FRIEND;
THERE'S A FINE, FINE LINE
BETWEEN REALITY AND PRETEND;
AND YOU NEVER KNOW TILL YOU REACH THE TOP

IF IT WAS WORTH THE UPHILL CLIMB.
THERE'S A FINE, FINE LINE BETWEEN LOVE
AND A WASTE OF TIME.

THERE'S A FINE, FINE LINE
BETWEEN A FAIRY TALE AND A LIE;
AND THERE'S A FINE, FINE LINE
BETWEEN "YOU'RE WONDERFUL" AND "GOOD-BYE."
I GUESS IF SOMEONE DOESN'T LOVE YOU BACK,
IT ISN'T SUCH A CRIME,
BUT THERE'S A FINE, FINE LINE BETWEEN LOVE
AND A WASTE OF YOUR TIME.

AND I DON'T HAVE THE TIME TO WASTE ON YOU ANYMORE.
I DON'T THINK THAT YOU EVEN KNOW WHAT YOU'RE LOOKING FOR.
FOR MY OWN SANITY, I'VE GOT TO CLOSE THE DOOR
AND WALK AWAY . . .
WHOA . . .

THERE'S A FINE, FINE LINE
BETWEEN TOGETHER AND NOT.
THERE'S A FINE, FINE LINE
BETWEEN WHAT YOU WANTED AND WHAT YOU GOT.
YOU'VE GOT TO GO AFTER THE THINGS YOU WANT
WHILE YOU'RE STILL IN YOUR PRIME . . .

THERE'S A FINE, FINE LINE BETWEEN LOVE
AND A WASTE OF TIME.

(On the screens, a counting video, which counts to fifteen—)

VIDEO

"Fifteen-Minute Intermission!"

Act Two

SCENE 1—PRINCETON'S APARTMENT / NEW YORK CITY

(PRINCETON's apartment is stacked high in pizza boxes, Chinese food containers, clothes, papers, and magazines. PRINCETON lies on top of the pile, wearing a robe, so lethargic he cannot move.)

PRINCETON

IT SUCKS TO BE ME.
IT SUCKS TO BE ME.
IT SUCKS TO BE SINGLE, UNEMPLOYED AND ALMOST . . .
God, I'm old.
23.
IT SUCKS TO BE ME.

(The BAD IDEA BEARS appear from behind the pile of junk.)

BAD IDEA BEARS

Hey, Princeton!

GIRL BEAR

We're here to cheer you up!

PRINCETON

Oh no!

BOY BEAR

Gosh, you look so blue! How about a little smile?

GIRL BEAR

I think I see a smile. I think I see a little smile. Aww, come on, Princeton!

PRINCETON

Sorry, guys, that's not going to work.

BOY BEAR

Judge Judy's your friend!

GIRL BEAR

Yeah, watch Judge Judy when you feel all sad and alone!

PRINCETON

It's not working.

BOY BEAR

Well, you could always hang yourself!

GIRL BEAR

Yeah! We found this rope!

PRINCETON

I'm not going to hang myself.

BAD IDEA BEARS

Awwwww.

PRINCETON

Would you guys go away?

BOY BEAR

Gosh, he's Snappy the Turtle today! We'll leave the rope just in case.

(*They leave the rope and disappear.*)

PRINCETON

Oh man.

(BRIAN *knocks and enters.*)

BRIAN

Princeton!

PRINCETON

Yeah.

BRIAN

Listen, buddy, nobody's seen you for two weeks. What's up with that?

PRINCETON

I went to work for a temp agency, and they fired me for being too depressing on the phone. I maxed out my cards. I'm two months behind in rent. I totally messed up my personal life. And Brian—I still haven't found my purpose!

(*A moment.*)

BRIAN

Wanna hear a joke?

PRINCETON

Sure.

BRIAN

So there's an octopus in line at the grocery store, and in his cart is a can of soup, a vibrator, and a redhead with gigantic tits.

(*A moment.*)

PRINCETON

Yeah?

BRIAN

I haven't figured out the punch line yet. Got any ideas?

(PRINCETON *moans and buries his head.*)

BRIAN

Man, what you need is a change of perspective. C'mon, let's go out and mess around in the city.

PRINCETON

No thanks.

BRIAN

I said come on, Princeton!

(*He smacks him on the head. Music starts.*)

BRIAN

Get off your ass and take a look around!
THERE IS LIFE OUTSIDE YOUR APARTMENT.
I KNOW IT'S HARD TO CONCEIVE

BUT THERE'S LIFE OUTSIDE YOUR APARTMENT,
AND YOU'RE ONLY GONNA SEE IT IF YOU LEAVE.
THERE IS COOL SHIT TO DO
BUT IT CAN'T COME TO YOU
AND WHO KNOWS, DUDE, YOU MIGHT EVEN SCORE!
THERE IS LIFE OUTSIDE YOUR APARTMENT
BUT YOU'VE GOT TO OPEN THE DOOR!

(CHRISTMAS EVE, TREKKIE, GARY, and NICKY enter and pick
PRINCETON up, dragging him outside.)

ALL BUT PRINCETON

THERE IS LIFE OUTSIDE
THERE IS LIFE OUTSIDE
THERE IS LIFE OUTSIDE
THERE IS LIFE OUTSIDE YOUR APARTMENT!
THERE'S A PIGEON SQUASHED ON THE STREET.

CHRISTMAS EVE

Ew.

GUYS EXCEPT PRINCETON

THERE'S A GIRL PASSING BY!

GARY

NO, I THINK IT'S A GUY!

ALL

AND A HOMELESS MAN WHO ONLY WANTS TO
BUY SOMETHING TO EAT!
Sorry! Can't help you!

(They enter the subway.)

ALL BUT PRINCETON
WE COULD GO TO THE ZOO!

TREKKIE MONSTER
PICK UP GIRLS AT NYU!

BRIAN
WE COULD SIT IN THE PARK SMOKING POT!

CHRISTMAS EVE
OR NOT!

ALL BUT PRINCETON
THERE IS LIFE OUTSIDE YOUR APARTMENT

PRINCETON
WELL, I GUESS I'LL GIVE IT A SHOT!

> (*Gunshot! Everybody screams.*
> *They arrive in Manhattan.*)

ALL
THERE IS LIFE OUTSIDE YOUR APARTMENT
I KNOW IT'S—
> (*A loud jackhammer—they cover their ears.*)
Christ!
THERE IS LIFE OUTSIDE YOUR APARTMENT

> (*They all look up in horror.*)

OFFSTAGE VOICE
I'm gonna jump!

ALL

Don't do it!

OFFSTAGE VOICE

Okay!

ALL

THERE IS COOL SHIT TO DO
BUT IT CAN'T COME TO YOU
SO COME—

> (*A car screeches to a halt.*)

VOICE

> (*Offstage.*)

Get out of the way, asshole!

PRINCETON

Fuck you! Ha-ha!

ALL

THERE IS LIFE OUTSIDE YOUR APARTMENT!
OH, YOU NEVER KNOW
WHAT'S AROUND THE BEND—
YOU COULD STEP IN DOG SHIT
OR MAKE A FRIEND!

> (LUCY *enters voluptuously. The guys turn to* PRINCETON.)

GUYS EXCEPT PRINCETON

TAKE HER HOME TO SEE YOUR APARTMENT!

LUCY

DO YOU WANNA FEEL SPECIAL?

ALL GUYS

SPECIAL!

LUCY

I CAN SEE THAT YOU DO.

ALL GUYS

OOH, OOH, DOOH WOW!

LUCY

WELL, I CAN MAKE YOU FEEL SPECIAL—

ALL GUYS

SPECIAL!

LUCY

IF YOU LET ME FEEL YOU.

ALL GUYS

SHE'LL FEEL YOU.

LUCY

WHERE'S YOUR PAD?

PRINCETON

NOT TOO FAR!

GUYS

WE COULD CALL YOU A CAR!

PRINCETON

WE'LL BE FINE! THANK YOU! SEE YA!

CHRISTMAS EVE

HOPE YOU DON'T GET GONORRHEA!

ALL

THERE IS LIFE OUTSIDE YOUR APARTMENT—

PRINCETON AND LUCY

BUT NOW IT'S TIME TO GO HOME!

(*Simultaneously:*)

GUYS	**PRINCETON and LUCY**
THERE IS LIFE OUTSIDE YOUR APARTMENT. THERE IS LIFE OUTSIDE YOUR APARTMENT. THERE IS LIFE OUTSIDE YOUR APARTMENT.	IT'S TIME TO GO HOME.
	PRINCETON
	IT'S TIME TO GO HOME.

LUCY	**TREKKIE**
I CAN MAKE YOU FEEL SPECIAL. LET ME MAKE YOU FEEL SPECIAL.	ME GOING HOME NOW, THAT'S WHERE ME GONNA GO! ME GOING HOME NOW, THAT'S WHERE ME GONNA GO! ME GOING HOME NOW, THAT'S WHERE ME GONNA GO!

ALL

BUT NOW IT'S TIME TO GO HOME!

TREKKIE MONSTER

FOR PORN!

(*Playoff.*)

SCENE 2 —ON THE AVENUE

(PRINCETON *heads toward his building as* KATE *exits her front door.*)

PRINCETON

Oh—hi, Kate!

KATE MONSTER

Good evening.

PRINCETON

I haven't seen you around.

KATE MONSTER

Mmm-hmmm.

(LUCY *enters, sultrily.*)

LUCY

You gonna show me upstairs?

PRINCETON

Sure, Lucy—um—one second, okay?

LUCY

Sure, baby. Don't let my motor idle too long.

(LUCY *enters the building.*)

KATE MONSTER

She a friend of yours?

PRINCETON

Yeah.

KATE MONSTER

Is her name "Purpose"?

PRINCETON

Listen, Kate, I gotta go.

KATE MONSTER

Have fun.

(PRINCETON *follows* LUCY *into his building.* KATE *is crushed.* CHRISTMAS EVE *enters.*)

CHRISTMAS EVE

What the matter, Kate Monster?

KATE MONSTER

I hate Princeton. He's with that Lucy.

CHRISTMAS EVE

Ohhh, that evil girl? She skanky. But that not make Princeton bad person, Kate Monster.

KATE MONSTER

I don't know anymore.

CHRISTMAS EVE

But you still feeling for him, don't you?

KATE MONSTER

(*Resigned.*)
I do feeling for him.

CHRISTMAS EVE

Sometimes person need time for learning. People always learning, all through their life. Look at momma bird. She push baby out of nest and that's it. If baby bird fly, good for baby. If baby bird fall and crack head on ground and get eaten by cat, then it need to do better next time.

KATE MONSTER

Why can't people get along and love each other, Christmas Eve?

CHRISTMAS EVE

You think getting along same as loving? Sometimes love right where you hating most, Kate Monster.
(*Sings.*)
THE MORE YOU RUV SOMEONE
THE MORE YOU WANT TO KILL 'EM.

KATE MONSTER

Ahhh.

CHRISTMAS EVE

THE MORE YOU RUV SOMEONE
THE MORE HE MAKE YOU CRY.
THOUGH YOU ARE TRY
FOR MAKING PEACE WITH THEM
AND RUVING,
THAT'S WHY YOU RUV SO STRONG

YOU LIKE TO MAKE HIM DIE.

THE MORE YOU RUV SOMEONE
THE MORE HE MAKE YOU CRAZY.
THE MORE YOU RUV SOMEONE
THE MORE YOU WISHING HIM DEAD!
SOMETIME YOU LOOK AT HIM AND ONLY SEE FAT AND RA-ZY.
AND WANTING BASEBALL BAT FOR HITTING HIM ON HIS HEAD!
RUV . . .

KATE MONSTER

LOVE . . .

CHRISTMAS EVE

AND HATE . . .

KATE MONSTER

AND HATE . . .

CHRISTMAS EVE

THEY LIKE TWO BROTHERS . . .

KATE MONSTER

BROTHERS . . .

CHRISTMAS EVE

WHO GO ON A DATE.

KATE MONSTER

WHO . . . WHAT?

CHRISTMAS EVE

WHERE ONE OF THEM GOES

OTHER ONE FOLLOWS.
YOU INVITING LOVE
HE ALSO BRINGING SORROWS.

KATE MONSTER

Ah, yes.

CHRISTMAS EVE

THE MORE YOU RUV SOMEONE
THE MORE YOU WANT TO KILL 'EM.
RUVVING AND KILLING
FIT LIKE HAND IN GLOVE!

SO IF THERE SOMEONE YOU ARE WANTING SO TO KILL 'EM,
YOU GO AND FIND HIM
AND YOU GET HIM
AND YOU NO KILL HIM
CAUSE CHANCES GOOD

KATE MONSTER AND CHRISTMAS EVE

HE IS YOUR/MY LOVE.

SCENE 3—KATE'S APARTMENT

(KATE *writes a message to* PRINCETON.)

KATE MONSTER

Dear Princeton. It was good to see you yesterday. Listen, I'm sorry
about what happened. But I'd love to do "friend" things with you.
I'm going to visit the viewing platform at the Empire State Building at
midnight tonight, and I'd love for you to come. Can you meet me there?

If not, please call and let me know. Otherwise, I guess I'll see you there!
Yours, Kate Monster.

(*On the screens, an instructional "counting" video. Five
nightstands appear.*)

CHILDREN'S VOICES

Five nightstands!

(*Four of them disappear. We zoom in.*)

ADULT VOICE

One nightstand.

(*We pull back to reveal a bedroom with something going on under
the covers.*)

ALL VOICES

ONE NIGHT STAND!

SCENE 4—PRINCETON'S APARTMENT

(*Lights rise in* PRINCETON*'s apartment.* LUCY *is wearing*
PRINCETON*'s robe. A knock on the door.*)

LUCY

Yeah?

KATE MONSTER

(*Entering, with an envelope.*)
Oh. It's you.

LUCY

Are you the cleaning lady?

KATE MONSTER

I will not rise to your bait. Where is Princeton?

LUCY

He's hosing off in the shower. You need something?

KATE MONSTER

I wanted to leave him this note, is all.

(*She puts the envelope on the window.*)

LUCY

Awww, man, that kid kept me busy all night. Say, baby, you mind checking to see if there are any scratch marks on my back?

KATE MONSTER

Oh, yes, I see them. It looks like they say, "Help Me."

(KATE *exits, slamming the door behind her.*)

LUCY

Hey, kid, you almost done in there?

PRINCETON

(*Offstage.*)
Yeah! I'm drying off!

LUCY

(*Picking up the note.*)
He doesn't need to be messing with some Monster.

(*She crinkles the note into a wad.*)

SCENE 5—THE AVENUE

(NICKY *and* BRIAN *enter from the side yard with beers.*)

NICKY

It's been a hard few weeks, Brian, what with Rod kicking me out, and I just want to say thank you for letting me stay with you and your lovely bride.

BRIAN

Actually, I wanted to talk to you about that—

(CHRISTMAS EVE *appears at the front door. She throws all of* NICKY*'s belongings out onto the sidewalk.*)

CHRISTMAS EVE

Brian, you tell him to *go*!

BRIAN

Honey, give me a minute—

CHRISTMAS EVE
(*To* NICKY.)

I no do your housework! I no cook for you and clean for you and pick up all your messing! One lazy fat ass plenty for this lady! This morning I take a shower and I pick up soap! And I say, "Who putting all these little green pubic hairs on soap?" They not belong to me. They not belong to Brian. Who then could it be? I about to puking! The welcome wagon go away! It gone!

(*She storms inside, swearing in Japanese.*)

BRIAN

Sorry, buddy.

NICKY

I don't know where to go!

BRIAN

You could stay with Princeton—or Kate—

NICKY

But I did already, and they kicked me out too!

BRIAN

There's gotta be someone who can help you out, buddy! Sorry!

(BRIAN *enters the building.*)

(GARY *enters, reading* Variety.)

NICKY

Oh! Why, good evening there, Gary!

GARY COLEMAN

Nicky!

NICKY

Gary, listen, I need a place to stay, and I was wondering if I could sleep on your floor until Rod and I patch things up.

GARY COLEMAN

I see. Well, how do I put this? No.

NICKY

No?! But I've asked *everyone*, and if you don't take me in, where will I live?

GARY COLEMAN

What about on the street?

NICKY

You mean, I should be homeless?

GARY COLEMAN

Sure!

NICKY

But that's a terrible way to live!

GARY COLEMAN

Look, kid, I know from living in the dumps. But look at the bright side—think of all the joy you'll bring to others when they find out just how miserable you are!

NICKY

What?

GARY COLEMAN

(*Sings.*)
RIGHT NOW YOU ARE DOWN AND OUT
AND FEELING REALLY CRAPPY.

NICKY

I'll say.

> **GARY COLEMAN**
> AND WHEN I SEE HOW SAD YOU ARE
> IT SORT OF MAKES ME HAPPY!

> **NICKY**

Happy?

> **GARY COLEMAN**
> SORRY, NICKY, HUMAN NATURE—
> NOTHING I CAN DO.
> IT'S SCHADENFREUDE!
> MAKING ME FEEL GLAD THAT I'M NOT YOU.

> **NICKY**

That's not very nice, Gary!

> **GARY COLEMAN**

I didn't say it was nice! But everybody does it.
> D'JA EVER CLAP WHEN A WAITRESS FALLS
> AND DROPS A TRAY OF GLASSES?

> **NICKY**

Yeah . . .

> **GARY COLEMAN**
> AND AIN'T IT FUN TO WATCH FIGURE SKATERS
> FALLING ON THEIR ASSES!

> **NICKY**

Sure!

> **GARY COLEMAN**
> DON'TCHA FEEL ALL WARM AND COZY

Ann Sanders, Kate Monster, and Sarah Stiles in the Broadway production.

(Photo © Carol Rosegg)

WARNING:
FULL PUPPET NUDITY

Avenue
Q
The Musical

Telecharge.com 212-239-6200 ▪ AvenueQ.com
Ⓖ Golden Theatre 252 W. 45th Street

'Avenue Q' has not been authorized or approved in any manner by The Jim Henson Company or Sesame Workshop, which have no responsibility for its content.

Lucy the Slut in an ad campaign for the Broadway production. (Photo by Nick Ruechel)

I am NOT a closeted HOMOWHATEVER!

The Musical

Telecharge.com 212-239-6200 ▪ AvenueQ.com

♿ Golden Theatre 252 W. 45th Street

'Avenue Q' has not been authorized or approved in any manner by The Jim Henson Company or Sesame Workshop, which have no responsibility for its content.

Rod. (Photo by Nick Ruechel)

'Avenue Q' has not been authorized or approved in any manner by The Jim Henson Company or Sesame Workshop, which have no responsibility for its content.

Kate Monster. (Photo by Nick Ruechel)

WHAT THE FUZZ
ARE YOU LOOKING AT?

Avenue
Q
The Musical

Telecharge.com 212-239-6200 ▪ AvenueQ.com
♿ Golden Theatre 252 W. 45th Street
'Avenue Q' has not been authorized or approved in any manner by The Jim Henson Company or Sesame Workshop, which have no responsibility for its content.

Trekkie Monster. (Photo by Nick Ruechel)

Tom Parsons, Boy Bear, Rachel Jerram, and Girl Bear in the Wyndham's Theatre production in London. (Photo © Catherine Ashmore / CM Ltd.)

Lucy the Slut and Delroy Atkinson in the Wyndham's Theatre production in London. (Photo © Catherine Ashmore / CM Ltd.)

Front: Rod and Paul Spicer. Rear, left to right: Delroy Atkinson, Siôn Lloyd, Nicky, Tom Parsons, Jacqueline Tate, Princeton, Kate Monster, Rachel Jerram, and Cassidy Janson in the Wyndham's Theatre production in London. (Photo © Catherine Ashmore / CM Ltd.)

WATCHING PEOPLE OUT IN THE RAIN?

NICKY

You bet!

GARY COLEMAN

THAT'S—

GARY AND NICKY

SCHADENFREUDE!

GARY COLEMAN

PEOPLE TAKING PLEASURE IN YO' PAIN!

NICKY

Schadenfreude? What's that, some kinda Nazi word?

GARY COLEMAN

Yup! It's German for "happiness at the misfortune of others!"

NICKY

"Happiness at the misfortune of others?" That is German!
   (*Sings.*)
WATCHING A VEGETARIAN
BEING TOLD SHE JUST ATE CHICKEN.

GARY COLEMAN

OR WATCHING A FRAT BOY REALIZE
JUST WHAT HE PUT HIS DICK IN!

NICKY

BEING ON AN ELEVATOR WHEN SOMEBODY SHOUTS, "HOLD THE
DOOR!"

GARY AND NICKY

NO!
SCHADENFREUDE!

GARY COLEMAN

"FUCK YOU, LADY, THAT'S WHAT STAIRS ARE FOR!"

BOTH

SCHADENFREUDE!
SCHADENFREUDE!

GARY COLEMAN

THE WORLD NEEDS PEOPLE LIKE YOU AND ME
WHO'VE BEEN KNOCKED AROUND BY FATE.
'CAUSE WHEN PEOPLE SEE US
THEY DON'T WANT TO BE US
AND THAT MAKES THEM FEEL GREAT!

NICKY

WE PROVIDE A VITAL SERVICE
TO SOCIETY!

GARY AND NICKY

YOU AND ME
SCHADENFREUDE!
MAKING THE WORLD A BETTER PLACE
MAKING THE WORLD A BETTER PLACE
MAKING THE WORLD A BETTER PLACE TO BE!

NICKY

Bye!

GARY COLEMAN

S-C-H-A-D-E-N-F-R-E-U-D-E!

SCENE 6—EMPIRE STATE BUILDING / STREET CORNER

(*The action crosscuts between* PRINCETON *and* LUCY *on a street corner, and* KATE MONSTER *atop the Empire State Building.*)

KATE MONSTER
All those people look like ants down there. And their hearts look about as tiny as the ones inside the men I've dated.
(*To the audience.*)
Princeton gave me this penny once. He said it was the symbol of his hopes and dreams. And he never called like I asked him to, and I don't see him anywhere, and pretty soon he'll be an hour late. If he comes at all.

(*On the street.* PRINCETON *sees* LUCY *and runs over.*)

PRINCETON
Hey—Lucy! Where'd you go this morning? I've been looking all over for you.

LUCY
Oh man. Why do I always get the "clingy" guys?

PRINCETON
Clingy? You left this morning without even saying good-bye!

LUCY
Listen, kid, sorry to be honest, but look at me. I can have my pick of the litter. If I want a relationship, I'll find a guy with a good job, who has

a future and a ton of money, and not some well-hung, baby-faced kid who leeches from his parents and can't get his act together.

PRINCETON
I think I heard a compliment in there somewhere—

(*On the Empire State Building.*)

KATE MONSTER
Well, that's how it feels to be stood up. I'm gonna get rid of this stupid penny. And I'll make a wish! I hope—more than anything, I hope I find someone who I love, someone who loves me back.
(*She tosses the penny.*)
Yaahhh!
(*Beat.*)
Somehow I don't feel any better.

(*On the street . . .*)

PRINCETON
But I'm only waiting for my purpose, Lucy! My break! My big revelation!

LUCY
You know the only revelation people have in life, kiddo? They're not special. *You're* not special. You're no luckier or more gifted than anyone else.

PRINCETON
You don't think so?

LUCY
No!

PRINCETON

Now whenever I pass by this place, I'll think about what you said just now.

LUCY

What's so special about this place?

PRINCETON

You mean here, on 34th and Fifth, right next to the Empire State Building?

> (*We hear a whistling sound, and a "thunk" as* LUCY's *body goes limp.*)

> (*A long moment.*)

PRINCETON

Lucy?

SCENE 7— THE HOSPITAL

> (*An EKG with "Lucy T. Slut" across the bottom. As the heart rate moves across the screen, it looks rather like two breasts.*)

> (PRINCETON *stands by* LUCY's *bed.*)

PRINCETON

Lucy, can you hear me?

> (KATE *rushes in.*)

KATE MONSTER

Princeton! I heard your friend had an accident! How is she?

PRINCETON

Her head fell off in the ambulance. The doctors spent all night sewing it back on, but the prognosis is good.

KATE MONSTER

What happened to her?

PRINCETON

Some idiot threw a penny off the Empire State Building.

(*A moment.*)

KATE MONSTER

Shit.

PRINCETON

What are you doing here?

KATE MONSTER

Why didn't you bother to say you weren't coming?

PRINCETON

Huh?

KATE MONSTER

I told you in my note—

PRINCETON

What note?

KATE MONSTER

The one I left with—
   (*She looks at* LUCY, *realizing.*)
Oh. I feel better now.

PRINCETON

How are you, Kate?

KATE MONSTER

Honestly?

PRINCETON

Of course!

KATE MONSTER

I'm working at Barnes and Noble. I miss my students. I work all day and I'm poorer than ever.

PRINCETON

What about your monster school?

KATE MONSTER

Some people's dreams come true, but I don't think I'm one of those people.

PRINCETON

Don't say that!

KATE MONSTER

But that's the way life is, Princeton. Nobody teaches you that when you're a kid, because if you knew, no one would ever dream. Or want to grow up. But you can't stop growing up.
   (*Beat.*)

I'm late for work.

    (PRINCETON *stops her.*)

PRINCETON

Kate, I wish you were happy, and I wish I had it together but I don't and I'm not sure when that's gonna happen. I'm sorry about hurting your feelings, because I think you're so special.
    (*A moment.*)
Sorry that wasn't more articulate.

KATE MONSTER

You were perfectly articulate.
    (*Beat.*)
I really do have to go.

    (*She exits. He looks after her.*)

    (*On the video screen, LUCY's EKG flatlines. A heavenly choir sings, and the EKG picks up again.*)

SCENE 8—ON THE AVENUE

    (NICKY *is on the Avenue.*)

NICKY

Help the homeless? Help the homeless?
    (ROD *enters.*)
Oh, hi, Rod!

ROD

Is that the wind I hear, rustling through the branches?

NICKY

Rod, listen, from now on I'll believe anything you say about yourself. And I apologize for being such a messy roommate. Now that I have a place of my own—behind that dumpster over there—I can appreciate how hard it is to keep things nice.

   (*No answer.*)

Rod, buddy, can you hear me?

   (*After a moment,* NICKY *exits.* ROD *looks after him sadly.*)

   (CHRISTMAS EVE *enters from her building.*)

CHRISTMAS EVE

You okay, Rod?

ROD

Christmas Eve, can I consult with you briefly?

CHRISTMAS EVE

Sure.

   (ROD *snuggles in her lap.*)

What your problem today?

ROD

It's tiny, really.

CHRISTMAS EVE

Go on—

ROD

I look at all my old friends who are married now, and I look at you and Brian—

CHRISTMAS EVE

Go on—

ROD

And I wonder—Why don't I have someone by my side, someone who makes me feel special, and safe? Someone who loves me the way I love them?

(*He begins to cry.*)

CHRISTMAS EVE

Rod, you special. Rod, you safe.

ROD

I miss Nicky.

CHRISTMAS EVE

I know you do.

SCENE 9—EMPIRE STATE BUILDING / A CORNER / THE HOSPITAL

(KATE *is on the Empire State Building.*)

KATE MONSTER

I WISH I COULD GO BACK TO COLLEGE
LIFE WAS SO SIMPLE BACK THEN.

(NICKY *appears on a dark corner, shivering.*)

NICKY

WHAT WOULD I GIVE

TO GO BACK AND LIVE
IN A DORM WITH A MEAL PLAN AGAIN!

(NICKY *and* KATE *sigh. The lights rise on* PRINCETON *at the
hospital, sitting next to* LUCY's *bed.*)

PRINCETON

I WISH I COULD GO BACK TO COLLEGE.
IN COLLEGE YOU KNOW WHO YOU ARE.
YOU SIT IN THE QUAD
AND THINK OH MY GOD
I AM TOTALLY GONNA GO FAR!

ALL

HOW DO I GO BACK TO COLLEGE?
I DON'T KNOW WHO I AM ANYMORE!

PRINCETON

I WANNA GO BACK TO MY ROOM
AND FIND A MESSAGE IN DRY-ERASE PEN ON THE DOOR!
OO-WHOA-OO-WHOA-OO
I WISH I COULD JUST DROP A CLASS . . .

NICKY

OR GET INTO A PLAY—

KATE MONSTER

OR CHANGE MY MAJOR—

PRINCETON

OR FUCK MY T.A.

ALL

I NEED AN ACADEMIC ADVISOR TO POINT THE WAY!
WE COULD BE . . .
SITTING IN THE COMPUTER LAB
4 A.M. BEFORE THE FINAL PAPER IS DUE
CURSING THE WORLD 'CUZ I DIDN'T START SOONER
AND SEEING THE REST OF THE CLASS THERE TOO.

I WISH I COULD GO BACK TO COLLEGE!
HOW DO I GO BACK TO COLLEGE?
AHHHHHHH. . . .

PRINCETON

I WISH I HAD TAKEN MORE PICTURES.

NICKY

BUT IF I WERE TO GO BACK TO COLLEGE
THINK WHAT A LOSER I'D BE
I'D WALK THROUGH THE QUAD,
AND THINK "OH MY GOD"—

ALL

"THESE KIDS ARE SO MUCH YOUNGER THAN ME."

SCENE 10—THE AVENUE

(NICKY *sees a bummed-out* PRINCETON.)

NICKY

Help the homeless! Help the—Hey, Princeton!

PRINCETON

Hi, Nicky.

NICKY

You look all down in the dumps.

PRINCETON

You could say that.

NICKY

Yeah, I'm in the dumps, too. I'm living there, in fact. Say, could you do something for me, buddy?

PRINCETON

Like what?

NICKY

Give me a quarter.

PRINCETON

Not right now, Nicky.

NICKY

Aww, come on, you know you want to! How 'bout a dime?

PRINCETON

I need a moment by myself, okay?

NICKY

You know what? You need to stop thinking about *yourself.* Try helping somebody else out for a change. Like me! Come on Princeton! Give me a quarter.

(*Sings.*)

HERE IN MY HAT.
YOU'LL FEEL BETTER—
IT'S EASY AS THAT!
HELPING OTHERS BRINGS YOU
CLOSER TO GOD,
SO GIVE ME A QUARTER!

PRINCETON

I don't have any change.

NICKY

Hmm.
OKAY,
GIVE ME A DOLLAR!

PRINCETON

That's not what I meant.

NICKY

GIVE ME A FIVE!

PRINCETON

Are you kidding?

NICKY

THE MORE YOU GIVE
THE MORE YOU GET—
THAT'S BEING ALIVE.
ALL I'M ASKING YOU
IS TO DO WHAT JESUS CHRIST WOULD DO.
HE'D GIVE ME A QUARTER.
WHY DON'T YOU?

PRINCETON

All right, all right, here you go.

(*He puts money in* NICKY*'s cup.*)

NICKY

Thanks!

PRINCETON

Take care.
(*A musical sting.*)
Whoa!

NICKY

What's the matter?

PRINCETON

I feel—generous! I feel—compassionate!

NICKY

And if you give me a twenty you'll feel even better!

PRINCETON

Helping other people out makes you feel fantastic! All this time I was running around thinking about me, me, me—and look where it's gotten me! Now I'm gonna do something for somebody else!

NICKY

Me?

PRINCETON

No—Kate! I'm going to raise the money to build that stupid Monster school she's always talking about!

NICKY

Okay.

PRINCETON

GIVE ME YOUR MONEY!

NICKY

What?!

PRINCETON

I NEED IT FOR KATE!

NICKY

I need it to eat!

PRINCETON

COME ON, NICKY—

NICKY

Get lost!

PRINCETON

IT'LL MAKE YOU FEEL GREAT!

NICKY

So would a burger!

PRINCETON

WHEN HER DREAM COMES TRUE
IT'LL ALL BE PARTLY THANKS TO YOU.
SO GIVE ME YOUR MONEY!

NICKY

I'd like to but I can't!

PRINCETON

GIVE ME YOUR MONEY!

NICKY

I'd like to but I need it!

PRINCETON

GIVE ME YOUR MONEY!

NICKY

I'd like to but I'm homeless! I can't! I need it! I'm homeless! I can't! I
need it! I'm homeless! I cant! I need it! I'm homeless!

    (PRINCETON *slaps* NICKY.)

Okay, here ya go.

PRINCETON

Thanks.

    (*A heavenly musical strain.* NICKY *is overcome by the spirit.*)

NICKY

SUDDENLY, I AM FEELING CLOSER TO GOD.
IT'S TIME TO STOP BEGGING,
IT'S TIME TO START GIVING!
WHAT CAN I GIVE TO ROD?
Something he'll like so much he'll take me back. I know! I'll find him a
boyfriend!

PRINCETON

That's the spirit!

PRINCETON and NICKY

WHEN YOU HELP OTHERS,
YOU CAN'T HELP HELPING YOURSELF!
WHEN YOU HELP OTHERS
YOU CAN'T HELP HELPING YOURSELF!

>   (BRIAN, GARY, *and* CHRISTMAS EVE *have entered.* PRINCETON
>   *and* NICKY *turn to them.*)

WHEN YOU HELP A MONSTER CHILD
YOUR ENDORPHINS WILL GO WILD!
WHEN YOU HELP OTHERS
YOU'RE REALLY HELPING YOURSELF!

GIVE US YOUR MONEY . . .

>   (*The same heavenly musical strain from before.* CHRISTMAS
>   EVE *and* GARY *put money in the hat, and react with shivers of
>   pleasure.*)

GARY COLEMAN

Hallelujah! I haven't felt this good since I sued my parents!

PRINCETON

I don't know how to thank you. Kate will be so grateful to you guys—I
mean, this kind of money is such a great start—

>   (CHRISTMAS EVE *has been counting the money in the hat.*)

CHRISTMAS EVE

Yes, six dollars!

PRINCETON

Six dollars? Is that all we got?

NICKY

Looks like we're gonna have to ask *more* people!

(*They turn to the audience.*)

ALL

GIVE US YOUR MONEY—
ALL THAT YOU'VE GOT!
JUST FORK IT ON OVER—

GARY COLEMAN

OR SOME PUPPETS WILL GET SHOT!

NICKY

Hey!

ALL

IT'S TIME TO PASS THE HAT

GARY COLEMAN

AND THERE'S NOTHING YOU CAN DO 'BOUT THAT!

(*They storm the audience.*)

ALL

SO
GIVE US YOUR MONEY!
GIVE US YOUR MONEY!
GIVE US YOUR MONEY!

WHEN YOU HELP OTHERS, YOU CAN'T HELP HELPING YOURSELF!
WHEN YOU HELP OTHERS, YOU CAN'T HELP HELPING YOURSELF!

EVERY TIME YOU DO GOOD DEEDS,
YOU'RE ALSO SERVING YOUR OWN NEEDS.
WHEN YOU HELP OTHERS, YOU'RE REALLY HELPING YOURSELF!

WHEN YOU GIVE TO A WORTHY CAUSE
YOU'LL FEEL AS JOLLY AS SANTA CLAUS!
WHEN YOU HELP OTHERS, YOU CAN'T
HELP
HELPING
YOURSELF!

(*Song ends.* PRINCETON *counts the money.*)

CHRISTMAS EVE

How much do we get?

PRINCETON

Well—besides this MetroCard, which I'm keeping—we have enough for—boy, it's not very much at all, is it?

CHRISTMAS EVE

Those people a bunch of cheapskates!

BRIAN

Never say never, Princeton, there's still one more person we need to hit up!

(TREKKIE *pops out of his window.*)

TREKKIE MONSTER

No! No! No! Go away. Me busy now.

CHRISTMAS EVE

But it for good cause!

BRIAN

Yeah, come on, Trekkie.

TREKKIE MONSTER

What in it for me? Now go away!

(*He turns back grumpily. They start to go.*)

PRINCETON

I guess Kate'll never get her school for Monsters.

TREKKIE MONSTER

(*Overhearing.*)
What you say?

BRIAN

Kate wants to open a school for Monsters.

TREKKIE MONSTER

School for Monsters? Me never hear of that!
(*Sings, emotionally.*)
SCHOOL FOR MONSTERS!
SCHOOL FOR LONELY LITTLE MONSTERS!
WHEN ME LITTLE, GOING TO SCHOOL
OTHER CHILDREN THINK ME NOT COOL,
POKING AND PULLING AT ME FUR.
NOW ME HAVE THERAPIST AND WORK ON THIS WITH HER.
BUT ME NO NEED ME THERAPY
IF MONSTER SCHOOL A REALITY!
Me be right back!

(He disappears for a moment, returns, and hurls two enormous
bags of money out the window.)
Me give you ten million dollars!

PRINCETON
(Dazzled.)
Trekkie! Where did you get all that money?

TREKKIE MONSTER
In volatile market, only stable investment is porn.

(He slams the window.)

ALL
WHEN YOU HELP OTHERS
YOU CAN'T HELP HELPING YOURSELF!
WHEN YOU HELP OTHERS
YOU CAN'T HELP HELPING YOURSELF!
EVERY TIME YOU DO GOOD DEEDS
YOU'RE ALSO SERVING YOUR OWN NEEDS.
WHEN YOU HELP OTHERS
YOU CAN'T
HELP
HELPING YOURSELF!

SCENE 11—ON THE AVENUE

(GARY, CHRISTMAS EVE, BRIAN, PRINCETON, and NICKY
surround KATE. They're looking at the abandoned middle building,
which has a sign hanging on it:
"Monsterssori School. Founder, Kate Monster.")

GARY COLEMAN

It's your school, Kate!

BRIAN

And here's a check with enough money to renovate the building!

CHRISTMAS EVE

And you can hire teachers, and cafeteria ladies, and make a real working school for Monsters! We all raised the money!

KATE MONSTER

You mean all that money, for me?

BRIAN

Most of it came from a donor who wishes to remain anonymous.

GARY COLEMAN

Let's just say, I chipped in too.

KATE MONSTER

I don't know what to say!

BRIAN

Just say "thanks!"

KATE MONSTER

Thank you! Thank you, everybody! The entire Monster community thanks all of you!

BRIAN

Listen, now that everybody's all gathered here, Christmas Eve and I have an announcement.

CHRISTMAS EVE

We getting divorced.

(*Everyone gasps.*)

I only kidding! But we leaving Avenue Q.

KATE MONSTER

What?

CHRISTMAS EVE

We married now. It time to move on. So we move to nicer neighborhood, to Flushing.

KATE MONSTER

But you can't leave!

BRIAN

Aw, come on, guys, we'll still keep in touch. And there's another reason: I'm starting a new career!

ALL

Yaaay!

BRIAN

Yeah—I'm a consultant!

CHRISTMAS EVE

I not know what that is but I so proud of him! And I have news too: I finally get a regular client! I a paid therapist!

NICKY

Who's your client?

CHRISTMAS EVE

Ohhhh, I not allowed to say. But I seeing him seven times a week at $250 an hour. He need a lot of help. But we work through his issues, and he come out other side as integrated person.

KATE MONSTER

I bet I know who it is.

CHRISTMAS EVE

He much better.

NICKY

You mean Rod?

CHRISTMAS EVE

I not allowed to say!

BRIAN

Say, where is he, anyway? Get him out here!

(*We hear a loud gunshot, offstage.*)

(*A horrified moment.*)

(*Everyone looks toward* ROD's *apartment.*)

CHRISTMAS EVE

Goddamn it.

(ROD *appears with an open champagne bottle.*)

ROD

Champagne for everybody! I've got some news!

CHRISTMAS EVE

Rod, you okay!

ROD

And you're okay, too.
(*He laughs.*)
Listen, everybody, I've confronted my fears and won, so I have a few things I'd like to say. Number one: I apologize for being so hotheaded and difficult. It was all because—and this is number two—hold your applause, everybody—I, Rod, am gay. SURPRISE!
(*No one responds.*)
Okay, and three. Nicky, I'm sorry. You're my best friend and I missed you so much. Will you move back in with me?

NICKY

If it makes you happy—

ROD

It would!

NICKY

(*Hugging* ROD.)
Hooray!

ROD

Oh, Nicky!

NICKY

Well, Rod, guess what I did? I put a personal ad all over the Internet with your picture on it!

ROD

You did *what*?

NICKY

And I found someone very special—

ROD

Nicky, no! I'm leaving!

> (NICKY *exits for a moment as* ROD *begins to hyperventilate.*)

KATE MONSTER

Okay, Rod: breathe, breathe—

> (NICKY *re-enters.*)

NICKY

Rod, I'd like you to meet—Ricky.

> (NICKY *enters. Well, someone who looks exactly like* NICKY, *but gay.*)

RICKY

Hey there, Rod buddy, it sure is nice to meet you!

NICKY

I think I know your type.

ROD

> (*Enraptured.*)

Oh, sweet suffering Jesus—Nicky! And Ricky!

> (*He turns, delighted, to the others.*)

My cup runneth over!

> (*Friskily.*)

Let's go!

(NICKY, ROD, *and* RICKY *exit excitedly,* ROD *laughing in hysterical joy.*)

GARY COLEMAN

Everybody's dreams are coming true, and then there's Gary Coleman.

BRIAN

Aw, come on, Gary.

KATE MONSTER

You've still got all of us!

GARY COLEMAN

(*To* CHRISTMAS EVE *and* BRIAN.)
Well, since you two are leaving, I better put that damn "For Rent" sign back up.

KATE MONSTER

(*Looking at her building.*)
The Monsterssori School. I don't even know where to start!

CHRISTMAS EVE

Do you know who get idea and collect all the money and buy building for you?

KATE MONSTER

Was it you?

CHRISTMAS EVE

No. It Princeton.

(KATE *turns to him.*)

KATE MONSTER

Princeton? For me?

PRINCETON

You said you couldn't make your dreams come true by yourself, so I shot for the stars.
>   (*Sings.*)
YOU'VE GOT TO GO AFTER THE THINGS YOU WANT
WHILE YOU'RE STILL IN YOUR PRIME—

KATE MONSTER

THERE'S A FINE, FINE LINE
BETWEEN LOVE—
Thank you, Princeton.

PRINCETON

So will you take me back?

KATE MONSTER

I'll be so busy now, with all of the contractors and inspections and hiring teachers and choosing textbooks—

PRINCETON

I can help you!

KATE MONSTER

Can we take it one day at a time?

>   (GARY *hangs up the "For Rent" sign. A young, optimistic-looking puppet appears.*)

NEWCOMER

>   (*Sings.*)

WHAT DO YOU DO
WITH A B.A. IN ENGLISH?
Oh, look! A "For Rent" sign!
     (*To* GARY.)
Oh my God! You're Gary Coleman!

GARY COLEMAN

Yes, I am!

NEWCOMER

Say, can you tell me where to find the super?

GARY COLEMAN

I am the super.

NEWCOMER

You're Gary Coleman and you're the super? Ha-ha-ha-ha-ha!

GARY COLEMAN

You laughing at me?

NEWCOMER

Sorry—sorry—

GARY COLEMAN

No, kid, it's all right. That's why I'm here.

(GARY *winks at the audience.*)

NEWCOMER

Listen—I wanna ask about the apartment for rent.

PRINCETON

Wait a minute! Wait a minute! That's it!

KATE MONSTER

What?

PRINCETON

(*Over dramatic, rising music.*)
My *purpose*! Look at this kid here, all fresh-faced and new and not knowing anything! He has no idea what he's in for! He thinks the hard part's over, but it's not! And maybe he needs some help! Maybe my purpose is to take everything I'm learning and put it—put it into a *show*!

(*A moment.*)

BRIAN

Are you high?

NEWCOMER

Yeah! And I'm not some young kid who doesn't know anything. Fuck you!

(*He exits.*)

PRINCETON

Why does everything have to be so hard?

GARY COLEMAN

Maybe you'll never find your purpose.

CHRISTMAS EVE

Lots of people don't.

PRINCETON
But then—I don't know why I'm even alive!

KATE MONSTER
Who does?
EVERYONE'S A LITTLE BIT UNSATISFIED.

BRIAN
EVERYONE GOES 'ROUND A LITTLE EMPTY INSIDE.

GARY COLEMAN
TAKE A BREATH
LOOK AROUND—

BRIAN
SWALLOW YOUR PRIDE—

KATE MONSTER
FOR NOW.

BRIAN, KATE, GARY, AND CHRISTMAS EVE
FOR NOW.

NICKY
NOTHING LASTS,

ROD
LIFE GOES ON,

NICKY
FULL OF SURPRISES.

ROD

YOU'LL BE FACED WITH PROBLEMS OF ALL SHAPES AND SIZES.

CHRISTMAS EVE

YOU'RE GOING TO HAVE TO MAKE A FEW COMPROMISES . . . FOR NOW.

TREKKIE MONSTER

FOR NOW.

ALL

BUT ONLY FOR NOW! (FOR NOW)
ONLY FOR NOW! (FOR NOW)
ONLY FOR NOW! (FOR NOW)
ONLY FOR NOW!

(LUCY *runs in, dressed modestly. She's bright and cheerful.*)

LUCY

Hey, everybody! I had to beat it from my Bible study to make it by the final number!

KATE MONSTER

Lucy? Is that you?

LUCY

A whole new me! I was saved by the Lord! And He gave me back my chastity—so I'm a virgin again!

(*The* BAD IDEA BEARS *appear.*)

GIRL BEAR

And we reformed our ways, too!

BOY BEAR

We found Scientology!

EVERYONE

Yaaaaaay!

LUCY

(*Sings.*)
FOR NOW WE'RE HEALTHY.

BRIAN

FOR NOW WE'RE EMPLOYED.

BAD IDEA BEARS

FOR NOW WE'RE HAPPY—

KATE MONSTER

IF NOT OVERJOYED.

PRINCETON

AND WE'LL ACCEPT THE THINGS WE CANNOT AVOID . . . FOR
NOW . . .

GARY COLEMAN

FOR NOW . . .

TREKKIE MONSTER

FOR NOW . . .

KATE MONSTER

FOR NOW . . .

ALL

BUT ONLY FOR NOW! (FOR NOW)
ONLY FOR NOW! (FOR NOW)
ONLY FOR NOW! (FOR NOW)

ONLY FOR NOW!
ONLY FOR NOW! (FOR NOW THERE'S LIFE!)
ONLY FOR NOW! (FOR NOW THERE'S LOVE!)
ONLY FOR NOW! (FOR NOW THERE'S WORK!)
FOR NOW THERE'S HAPPINESS!
BUT ONLY FOR NOW! (FOR NOW DISCOMFORT!)
BUT ONLY FOR NOW! (FOR NOW THERE'S FRIENDSHIP!)
ONLY FOR NOW (FOR NOW!)
ONLY FOR NOW!

ONLY FOR NOW! (SEX!)
IS ONLY FOR NOW! (YOUR HAIR!)
IS ONLY FOR NOW! (GEORGE BUSH!)
IS ONLY FOR NOW!
DON'T STRESS, RELAX, LET LIFE ROLL OFF YOUR BACKS.
EXCEPT FOR DEATH AND PAYING TAXES,
EVERYTHING IN LIFE IS ONLY FOR NOW!

NICKY

EACH TIME YOU SMILE—

ALL

. . . ONLY FOR NOW

KATE MONSTER

IT'LL ONLY LAST A WHILE.

ALL

. . . ONLY FOR NOW

PRINCETON

LIFE MAY BE SCARY

ALL

. . . ONLY FOR NOW—
BUT IT'S ONLY TEMPORARY.
    (*Everyone but* PRINCETON *makes their way offstage.*)
BA-DUM BA-DUM, BA-DUM BA-DUM
BA-DUM BA-DUM BA-DA DA DA DA
BA-DA DA-DA DA DA-DA
BA-DUM BA-DA, BA-DUM BA-DA, OOOOO—

PRINCETON

EVERYTHING IN LIFE IS ONLY FOR NOW.

    (PRINCETON *goes to his door, turns, and looks at the Avenue.*)

    (*The end.*)

AFTERWORD

The script in the preceding pages does not represent a finished show, even seven-plus years after *Avenue Q*'s first appearance on a New York stage. *Avenue Q* has always been a living organism, still evolving even on the day of this writing.

The changes certainly came swiftly in our month of previews Off-Broadway in early 2003. Our stage managers grew accustomed to a blizzard of pages arriving on a daily basis. Scenes were tightened, cut, or rewritten top to bottom; jokes were honed, lyrics sharpened. After that run, many more changes arrived when we moved to Broadway's Golden Theater in July.

We thought we might rest easy then, but we had a run in Las Vegas, and, well, Bobby and Jeff thought "Schadenfreude" might land even better if they cut a small section, and I'd dreamed up a joke for Brian involving a vibrator and an octopus, and then Bobby and Jeff imagined a new opening to the second act. So a small flurry of further changes entered the show.

Then for London, we tried some adjustments to make the show more accessible to the U.K. audience. We realized they got the show just fine in its original form, so we changed most of the changes back. But small Americanisms remained altered just for London, like "folks" (which became "parents") and "Korean deli" (which became "Chinese restaurant"). Overall tightening and smoothing continued, and then we added even more changes when we began the first national tour. And all of these alterations slowly filtered out to the other running companies, though I don't believe there was ever a moment when they were all doing exactly the same show.

We made some of the changes to keep up with the times. Originally, Brian and Christmas Eve moved to the Lower East Side at show's end. But as *Avenue Q* continued its run, that neighborhood grew ever *chic*-er. So we changed it to Hell's Kitchen for some of the *Q* companies – a neighborhood that *sounded* threatening, but then the day came when Hell's Kitchen also became trendy. Another change was in order! Brian and Christmas Eve's current destination is Flushing, Queens. (Investment tip: buy property in Flushing immediately, as it's bound to become the hot new place to live.)

Avenue Q officially opened Off-Broadway on March 20, 2003, the night the United States military began the Iraq invasion. To speak out against George Bush was frowned upon by nearly everyone in the media, even so-called "liberal" media outlets, so our final "George Bush (is only for now!)" received a deafening response from audiences thirsty for any hint of irreverence toward that particular leader. Certainly we got some complaints. But the line is actually a statement of simple fact, and we always felt it revealed more about the audience than anything.

As discontent with the president grew over the years, the response to that line actually became more muted. And after he left office, a small controversy erupted as we struggled to find a fitting replacement. Nothing worked as well in that difficult two-syllable window. "Fox News" came close, though. Then BP began the process of destroying the Gulf Coast with an oil disaster that continues as of this writing. The use of their initials in "For Now" finally returned us to that vigorous audience response. For now. (We leave "George Bush" as a tribute in this version of the script.)

After "The Money Song," as Princeton peeks in the hat for the contributions of the audience, he always finds something "local" there. In New York, he finds a Metrocard. In Las Vegas, he found a ticket stub to "The Thunder From Down Under," a male-stripper review. On the national tours, the actor playing Princeton kept track of local sports teams so Princeton could "find" their respective ticket stubs.

When our London run began, Princeton discovered a euro and noted: "That won't buy us anything!" A few years later, as the pound declined against the euro, Cameron Mackintosh suggested we switch the reference to the British pound, and we did. We kept the follow-up line—"That won't buy us anything!"—and the audience roared.

One difficult series of changes occurred when Gary Coleman tragically passed away on May 28, 2010, just over a month ago as of this writing. Though we never made him say anything we thought he wouldn't want to say himself, some of his lines came off as rather dark in light of his death. Some rapid changes went into the script on a short-term basis, and then nearly everything returned over the ensuing weeks. Some who haven't seen the show imagine that ours is a mockery of Gary, but he lives on in *Avenue Q* as a plucky and wise survivor, loved and valued by his friends. Not a great deal of alteration was necessary.

Today I redlined the script for publication, and I found a single word I'd always considered deleting. So I did. I'm not going to tell you what it is. I may give the change to the stage managers of our currently running companies. Or it may just exist here.

I guess I hope that Bobby and Jeff and I will always keep rejiggering and tinkering and making the show better. *Avenue Q* changed our lives, after all, and continues to do so. Why shouldn't we return the favor?

Jeff Whitty
July 2010

BIOGRAPHIES

ROBERT LOPEZ (Music and Lyrics, Original Concept) won the 2004 Tony Award (with Jeff Marx) for Best Score for *Avenue Q*. Upcoming projects include *The Book of Mormon* (heading for Broadway in 2011, co-written with Trey Parker and Matt Stone, creators of *South Park*), and, with his wife Kristen Anderson-Lopez, songs for Disney Animation's *Winnie the Pooh* (2011), and *Up Here*, a musical romantic comedy commissioned by the Roundabout Theatre Company. He won Daytime Emmy Awards in 2008 and 2010 for his music for Nick Jr.'s *The Wonder Pets*. He earned a 2007 Primetime Emmy nomination for his and Jeff Marx's musical episode of NBC's *Scrubs*. His musical version of *Finding Nemo* (2007), co-written with Kristen Anderson-Lopez, is currently playing in Disney's Animal Kingdom in Walt Disney World.

JEFF MARX (Music and Lyrics, Original Concept) never intended to be a writer. He was a musical theater performing major in college, but they told him he'd never make it as an actor and he believed them. It was devastating at the time, but it turned out all right. He went on to law school, passed the New York Bar exam, and started looking for clients in the entertainment industry in New York City. He joined the BMI Musical Theater Workshop, thinking it would be a great place to network and meet talented young writers he could represent. But one thing led to another, he met Bobby there, they started writing songs together, and they wrote a spec script for a Muppet movie, which they submitted to the Jim Henson Company. When Henson turned it down, Jeff and Bobby said, "Fuck the Muppets, let's create our own fucking Muppets," and they started inventing *Avenue Q*. When that took off, he stopped looking for law clients.

JEFF WHITTY (Book) won the 2004 Tony Award for Best Book of a Musical for *Avenue Q*, which has been performed On- and Off-Broadway, on tour, and in dozens of international productions. Other musicals include *Tales of the City* (scored by Jake Shears and John Garden of the Scissor Sisters) and *Bring It On: The Musical* (music by Tom Kitt and Lin-Manuel Miranda, lyrics by Amanda Green and Lin-Manuel Miranda). Plays include *The Further Adventures of Hedda Gabler*, *The Hiding Place*, *Suicide Weather*, *The Plank Project*, and *Balls*. Theaters producing his work include the Oregon Shakespeare Festival, the Atlantic Theater Company, the Vineyard Theater, the New Group, Actors Conservatory Theatre (San Francisco), the Alliance Theater (Atlanta), and South Coast Repertory (Costa Mesa). Whitty is also an actor, having performed Off-Broadway, regionally, and in wee bits on film and TV. He wishes to thank the O'Neill Theater Center for their role in developing *Avenue Q* and *Tales*.

Find your purpose...

Avenue

...do it on stage.

Performance rights for *Avenue Q* are available exclusively from Music Theatre International.

To license *Avenue Q* for your own theatre, view photos and production tips from other productions, and check out our great additional resources designed to help make producing *Avenue Q* easier, visit us online at **www.mtishows.com**.

MTI MUSIC THEATRE INTERNATIONAL

421 west 54th street • new york, ny 10019 • 212.541.4684 • www.mtishows.com